ACCOUNTING
AN INTERNATIONAL
PERSPECTIVE

ACCOUNTING

AN INTERNATIONAL PERSPECTIVE

Fifth Edition

Helen Gernon
University of Oregon

Gary K. Meek
Oklahoma State University

Boston   Burr Ridge, IL   Dubuque, IA   Madison, WI
New York   San Francisco   St. Louis
Bangkok   Bogotá   Caracas   Lisbon   London   Madrid   Mexico City
Milan   New Delhi   Seoul   Singapore   Sydney   Taipei   Toronto

McGraw-Hill Higher Education

A Division of The McGraw-Hill Companies

ACCOUNTING: AN INTERNATIONAL PERSPECTIVE

Published by Irwin/McGraw-Hill, an imprint of The McGraw-Hill Companies, Inc. 1221 Avenue of the Americas, New York, NY, 10020. Copyright © 2001, 1997, 1994, 1991, 1987, by The McGraw-Hill Companies, Inc. All rights reserved. No part of this publication may be reproduced or distributed in any form or by any means, or stored in a database or retrieval system, without the prior written consent of The McGraw-Hill Companies, Inc., including, but not limited to, in any network or other electronic storage or transmission, or broadcast for distance learning.

Some ancillaries, including electronic and print components, may not be available to customers outside the United States.

This book is printed on acid-free paper.

1 2 3 4 5 6 7 8 9 0 FGR/FGR 0 9 8 7 6 5 4 3 2 1 0

ISBN 0072316381

Page 74: FASB Statement No. 131, *Disclosures about Segments of an Enterprise and Related Information,* is copyrighted by the Financial Accounting Standards Board, 401 Merritt 7, P.O. Box 5116, Norwalk, Connecticut 06856-5116, U.S.A. Portions are reprinted with permission. Complete copies of this document are available from the FASB.

Publisher: *Jeffrey J. Shelstad*
Sponsoring editor: *Stewart Mattson*
Editorial assistant: *Erin Cibula*
Marketing manager: *Richard Kolasa*
Project manager: *Susanne Riedell*
Production associate: *Gina Hangos*
Coordinator freelance design: *Mary L. Christianson*
Supplement coordinator: *Mark Sienicki*
Media technology producer: *Ed Przyzycki*
Freelance cover designer: *Tin Box Studios, Inc.*
Cover photograph: © *PhotoDisc/background series 22*
Compositor: *GAC Indianapolis*
Typeface: *10/12 Times Roman*
Printer: *Quebecor Printing Book Group/Fairfield*

Library of Congress Cataloging-in-Publication Data

Gernon, Helen Morsicato, 1946–
    Accounting : an international perspective / Helen Gernon, Gary K. Meek.—5th ed.
    p. cm.
    Rev. ed. of: Accounting, 4th ed. / Gerhard G. Mueller, Helen Gernon, Gary K. Meek. c1997.
    Includes index.
    ISBN 0-07-231638-1 (softcover)
    1. International business enterprises—Accounting. 2. Comparative accounting. 3.
    Accounting—Standards. I. Meek, Gary K., 1949– II. Title.
    HF5686.I56 G47 2001
    657'.96—dc21
                                                                    00-027785
www.mhhe.com

We dedicate this book to Gerhard G. Mueller

We enter the 21st century knowing that global events will increasingly affect our lives. Around the world, trade barriers are falling and whole industries are being deregulated. Democracy is spreading—increasing individual choice—and market capitalism has been embraced as the reigning economic model. Capital is mobile and capital markets are becoming global. As one report has stated, globalization "is a reality, not a choice." Driving this global transformation are computerization and telecommunications. Indeed, new technology makes the internationalization of product and finance markets possible. Corporations, too, are making themselves over to adapt to the global economy. Flexibility is the key as more and more of them reorganize as networks and stress interdependent alliances and strategic partnerships with other companies, rather than self-sufficiency in all areas. Information, including accounting information, is a critical resource in these makeovers, supporting the linkages both internally and with the outside world.

This book is dedicated to the proposition that the international dimension of accounting is an integral part of the subject. Students who do not learn about it have not been adequately prepared for the world they will soon enter. Thus, your authors believe that the study of accounting is incomplete without considering its international aspects. The book provides a general, nontechnical overview of the subject matter of international accounting.

This book is also a testament to the positive influence of research on teaching. It is sometimes said that academic research has little or nothing to do with what goes on in the classroom. However, this book is largely a synthesis of international accounting research. Nearly everything we say in this book is based on research findings over the past 35 years or so. Thus, as the material is taught in the classroom, research findings are directly transferred to students of accounting.

CONTENTS AND CHANGES IN THE FIFTH EDITION

The book contains 10 chapters. The first six deal with financial accounting issues. Chapter 1 discusses the factors that influence the development of financial accounting practices and that, therefore, explain the similarities and differences in financial accounting around the world. Chapter 2 describes the important areas of difference in worldwide financial accounting practices. Institutional efforts to harmonize accounting diversity are the subject of Chapter 3, while Chapter 4 discusses the ways multinational corporations report to financial statement users in other countries. Chapter 5 focuses on disclosure trends, notably some innovative disclosures coming from Europe. Finally, Chapter 6 deals with consolidations and foreign currency translation. International financial statement analysis is the subject of Chapter 7. It bridges into the next three chapters—Chapters 8 through 10—which deal with managerial accounting issues. Chapter 8 is about information systems for multinational planning and control, while Chapter 9 discusses performance evaluation in multinationals. The interrelated topics of international taxation and multinational transfer pricing are covered in Chapter 10. Throughout these 10 chapters, we also identify and discuss what we believe to be important emerging issues in international accounting.

Every chapter starts with the enumeration of five specific learning objectives. At the end of each chapter are review questions, designed to reinforce chapter material; several short cases that integrate, and sometimes extend, the material; and a list of additional readings for those who wish to delve further into the subjects. Some of the readings are fairly easy, while others are more difficult.

An *Instructor's Manual* accompanies this book. It contains chapter outlines, solutions to the study questions and cases, and an exam bank with answers. We also offer suggestions on how to use this book. The *Instructor's Manual* is designed to be user friendly, with the expressed intention of making *Accounting: An International Perspective* as easy to use as possible.

The Fifth Edition adds many new illustrations from MNC annual reports and the professional international accounting literature. Each chapter has been rewritten, adding and deleting to reflect the current state of the art of the field of international accounting. The entire text has been thoroughly updated.

The book can be used in several ways. Depending on the level and length of the course, it can stand alone or be supplemented with additional readings or cases. The chapters are modularized so the teacher can pick and choose among them or use them in different order than they are presented here. Given its nontechnical nature, *Accounting: An International Perspective* has the flexibility to be used in courses aimed at accounting and nonaccounting students alike. It can be used in upper-division undergraduate and graduate (especially introductory MBA) courses. The book can also be used for a short course in international accounting. And, it can still be used as a supplement to add an international dimension for students taking the first-year course in accounting. By incorporating the chapters throughout the year, financial and managerial topics can be "internationalized" in an integrative way. Finally, faculty, graduate students, practicing professional accountants, and financial executives might use the book to gain a quick overview of the international dimensions of the accounting discipline.

CONCLUSION

Previous editions of this book, coauthored with Gerhard G. Mueller, have enjoyed considerable acceptance worldwide. Our book has been translated into Japanese, Korean, Russian, and Spanish. We thank Gerry for the opportunity to work with him on earlier editions. Even though he is no longer involved in writing this book, his vision and ideas continue to shape it. That is why we dedicate this Fifth Edition to Gerry Mueller, our friend and colleague.

All sins of omission or commission are to be debited to the authors. Comments from users will be credited—gladly and without deferral. We hope to hear from you if you have occasion to use this book.

Helen Gernon

Gary K. Meek

C O N T E N T S

ACCOUNTING

AN INTERNATIONAL
PERSPECTIVE

1

AN INTERNATIONAL PERSPECTIVE ON FINANCIAL ACCOUNTING

LEARNING OBJECTIVES

1. Demonstrate how accounting is influenced by its environment and responds to the information needs of those who use it.

2. Understand the link between accounting and the global economy.

3. Explain the major environmental variables that shape accounting development.

4. Show that accounting around the world is different to the extent that business environments are different, and similar, to the extent that they are similar.

5. Identify and explain the three major accounting "models" in the world—fair presentation/full disclosure, legal compliance, and inflation-adjusted.

Accounting provides economic information about various types of enterprises that is useful for making decisions about resource allocations. *Financial* accounting information is oriented primarily toward those parties external to the business enterprise who provide capital to it. Those who have funds to invest or lend may decide where to place their resources based on the *financial reports* (i.e., financial accounting information) that business enterprises prepare. Exhibit 1–1 illustrates this relationship between business enterprises and capital providers. Accounting exists because it satisfies a need—in particular, a need for information. And in

---

EXHIBIT 1–1   Financial Accounting Information and Capital Resources Flows

---

```
                           ─── $ ───
   ┌──────────┬──────────┐        ┌──────────┬──────────┐
   │ Resource │ users    │        │ Resource │ providers │
```

Resource | users   Resource | providers

┌─────────────────────────┐   ┌─────────────────────────┐
│   │   │   Providers of   │
│   Business   │   │   capital   │
│   enterprises   │   │ (shareholders, creditors,│
│   │   │   government)   │
└─────────────────────────┘   └─────────────────────────┘

Information | providers   Information | users

                   Financial
                   accounting
                   information

---

order to be relevant to the resource providers, accounting information must be responsive to their needs.

ACCOUNTING AND THE ENVIRONMENT

Accounting is shaped by the environment in which it operates. Just as nations have different histories, values, and political systems, they also have different patterns of financial accounting development. For example, accounting as studied by students in the United States is not the same accounting that students in other countries study. Indeed, diversity is what we see. This diversity is an outgrowth of the variety of business environments around the world and the fact that accounting is environmentally sensitive. It is interesting to note that when countries' business environments are similar, their financial accounting systems also tend to be similar. Moreover, as national economies become more interdependent and converge into a global economy, so too is there some convergence of accounting around the world.

In many countries (such as the United States) financial accounting information is directed primarily toward the needs of shareholders, and "decision usefulness" is the overriding criterion for judging its quality. However, in other countries, financial accounting has a different focus and performs other roles. For example, in some countries financial accounting is designed primarily to ensure that the proper amount of income tax is collected by the national government. This is the case in many South American countries. In other countries financial accounting is designed to help accomplish macroeconomic policies, such as achieving a predetermined rate of growth in the nation's economy. Whether income tax and economic policy information is also useful to individual shareholders and creditors is somewhat beside the point.

The consequences of financial accounting differences are all around us. They are reflected in the relative popularity of accounting as a major for university studies, and in the numbers of people with accounting backgrounds becoming senior government officials or top corporate executives. There is a different national emphasis on the use of accounting information in assessing environmental damage liabilities and especially in regulating public securities markets.

VARIABLES SHAPING ACCOUNTING DEVELOPMENT

External Finance

The Industrial Revolution in the United States and Britain created a tremendous amount of new wealth in these countries—wealth that spread widely among the general populace. As companies grew, their needs for capital also grew, and the rising middle class became a source of much of this needed capital. What emerged from this phenomenon had an important impact on financial accounting in these two countries. First, the shareholder group became large and diverse, and companies acquired a widespread ownership (i.e., many shareholders). Second, the owners became divorced from the management of their companies, and the professional, nonowner manager developed. Investors became essentially uninvolved in the day-to-day running of the companies they owned.

In such an environment, financial accounting information becomes an important source of information about how well a company is doing. Since it is impractical for the many shareholders to directly contact company management or to personally inspect the accounting records, the professional managers provide financial reports to investors in order to communicate their stewardship over the resources entrusted to them. With such a relationship, it is hardly surprising that financial accounting is primarily oriented toward the information needs of shareholders. Financial accounting in Britain and the United States has had such an orientation for many years. Moreover, these countries have large and developed stock markets. As a result, a great deal of information is disclosed in companies' financial reports; and determining profitability (i.e., management performance) is an objective of financial accounting. Enabling investors to predict the company's future cash flows is another objective.

Other countries (such as Switzerland, Germany, and Japan), have credit-based systems. Here, the environment is characterized by a few, very large banks that satisfy most of the capital needs of business. Ownership also tends to be concentrated. There are close ties between companies and banks and relationships are long term. The information needs of the resource providers are satisfied in a relatively straightforward way—through personal contacts and direct visits. Since the business enterprises have to deal with only a few creditors—and maybe even just one—direct access is an efficient and practical way to have the company's financial health monitored. The national governments require some public disclosure, and so companies still prepare financial reports. Not surprisingly, though, they tend not to contain as much information as, say, U.K. companies' reports. And since banks are the primary source of capital, financial accounting is oriented toward creditor protection. One sees, for example, such practices as conservatively valuing assets and overvaluing liabilities in order to provide a "cushion" for the bank in the event of default. These practices also reduce the dividend demands of shareholders.

France and Sweden offer still another orientation of financial accounting. National government plays a strong role in managing the country's resources, and business enterprises are expected to accomplish the government's policies and macroeconomic plans. Governments also actively ensure that businesses have adequate capital and will lend or even invest in companies if necessary. Financial accounting is oriented toward decision making by government planners. Firms follow uniform accounting procedures and reporting practices, which facilitate better government decisions.

Of course, the relationship between a business enterprise and providers of business capital changes quite drastically when new capital is secured in international financial markets. Then the information demands of both domestic and international sources of finance have to be satisfied, which typically means going beyond national expectations and customs in providing financial reports. This topic is explored later in this chapter and in Chapter 4.

In summary, external finance has an impact on the orientation of financial accounting as follows:

1. Who the providers of capital—the information users—are (for example, shareholders, banks, or the government).
2. How many investors and creditors there are.
3. How close the relationship is between businesses and the providers of capital.
4. How developed the stock exchanges and bond markets are.
5. The extent of use of international financial markets.

Legal System

Many dichotomize the accounting world into those countries with a "legalistic" orientation toward accounting and those with a "nonlegalistic" orientation. The legalistic approach to accounting is predominantly represented by so-called code law countries, and the preponderance of countries with a nonlegalistic approach are the so-called common law countries. Laws in code law countries are a series of "thou shalts" that stipulate the minimum standard of behavior expected. Citizens are obligated to comply with the letter of the law. In most code law countries, accounting principles are national laws; that is, accounting practices are codified much as the tax code is in the United States. Thus, financial accounting is very much a public-sector activity, administered by governmental (or quasi-governmental) bodies. Accounting practices and rules tend to be highly prescriptive, detailed, and procedural. Also, a primary role of financial accounting in these countries is to determine how much income tax a company owes the government. Argentina, France, and Germany have legalistic approaches to accounting.

The nonlegalistic approach is usually found in common law countries. Laws are a series of "thou shalt nots" that establish the limits beyond which it is illegal to venture. Within these limits, however, latitude and judgment are permitted and encouraged. Accounting practices in common law countries are largely determined by accountants themselves (i.e., in the private sector), and they evolve by becoming commonly accepted in practice. Thus accounting tends to be more adaptive and innovative. The United Kingdom and the United States are common law countries.

Political and Economic Ties with Other Countries

Accounting technology is imported and exported just as political systems and ideologies are, and countries have similar accounting for this reason. The United States has influenced accounting in Canada due to geographic proximity and close economic ties and because a number of Canadian companies routinely sell shares of common stock or borrow money in the United States. The United States is Mexico's principal trading partner; and, also because of proximity, accounting in Mexico is very much like that in the United States.[1] As a former protectorate of the United States, the Philippines has similar accounting requirements. Finally, accounting in Israel is heavily influenced by U.S. accounting practices as a result of the historical and sociological ties between the two nations.

Another significant force in worldwide accounting has been the United Kingdom, principally England and Scotland. Almost every former British colony has an accounting profession and financial accounting practices patterned after the U.K. model. These countries include Australia, New Zealand, Malaysia, Pakistan, India, and South Africa. The British not only exported their brand of accounting but also "exported" many accountants. (In fact, Britain is the only major former colonial power to transfer both its accounting ideas and its accountants.) Most early "U.S." accountants also came from Britain, seeking the job opportunities associated with the economic expansion that was occurring in the United States around the turn of the 20th century. Former colonies of France and Germany have been similarly influenced by their respective "mother countries," though not quite so profoundly as those of the United Kingdom.

Since the early 1970s, the European Union (EU) has been attempting to harmonize the accounting practices of its 15 member states. Recall from our earlier discussion that Britain, Germany, and France have fundamentally different

---

[1]The North American Free Trade Agreement (NAFTA) will further integrate already existing Canadian, U.S., and Mexican accounting similarities.

orientations about the role and purpose of financial accounting. However, as European allies and members of the EU, they have a number of similar economic interests, and they are seriously attempting to bring their accounting practices closer together.

Political and economic ties among nations shape their accounting development; thus, one cannot help but wonder whether the world's growing economic interdependence will force accounting practices to become more similar. Indeed, this type of thinking has given rise to the international accounting standards movement. As explored more fully in Chapter 3, the International Accounting Standards Committee (IASC) has become the driving force worldwide to develop international financial accounting standards and seek their widest possible acceptance and use. The International Federation of Accountants (IFAC), among many other activities, develops and issues international auditing standards (also see Chapter 3), which were accepted in 1992 for financial reporting in international financial markets. In Europe, accounting *Directives* are issued by the EU and are incorporated into the national corporate legislation of all EU member countries in due course. Many world agencies like the United Nations (UN), the Organization for Economic Cooperation and Development (OECD), the Association of South East Asian Nations (ASEAN), and the International Monetary Fund (IMF) have operating units specifically concerned with international financial standard setting and reporting. The internationalization of our political and economic environments is directly driving the internationalization of accounting.

Levels of Inflation

Accounting in many countries (including the United States) is based in part on the *historical cost principle*. This principle is itself based on an assumption that the currency unit used to report financial results is reasonably stable. In other words, the historical cost principle assumes that the dollar (for U.S. companies) does not change in value—that there is little or no inflation. As one might expect the less realistic this assumption becomes, the greater the strain on the historical cost principle.

Briefly, the historical cost principle means that companies originally record sales, purchases, and other business transactions at transaction prices and make no adjustments to these prices later. Generally speaking, the historical cost principle affects accounting most significantly in the area of asset values, mainly those assets (such as land and buildings) that the company keeps for a long time. Obviously, the reasonableness of the historical cost principle varies inversely with the level of inflation. Germany and Japan, two of the staunchest adherents to the historical cost principle, have historically experienced very little inflation. However, some South American countries, ravaged by inflation problems for years, long ago abandoned any attachment to strict historical cost. Companies in these countries routinely write up the values of their assets based on changes in general price levels.

The United States experienced very little inflation in the post-World War II era until the 1970s. Most U.S. accountants were happy with historical cost accounting, and interest in adjusting for changes in price levels was mainly confined to a few academicians. However, once inflation became persistent and high (at least by U.S. standards), interest in measuring the effects of price-level changes on business enterprises began to grow. In 1979 the Financial Accounting Standards Board (FASB), the organization that determines acceptable accounting practices for U.S. companies, required the largest U.S. firms to experiment with ways to account for changes in prices. Eventually, these firms had to report the effects of changing prices in their published annual reports and in filings with the Securities and Exchange Commission (SEC). However, this requirement was rescinded in 1984 as inflation levels in the United States returned to more modest levels.

Interest in incorporating the effects of changing prices into a company's accounting records waxes and wanes with the degree that a country is affected by inflation. Countries with a long history of inflation have already done something about it, while those with low inflation do not even consider abandoning historical cost. Some of the most novel ideas dealing with inflation accounting were proposed in Europe during the 1920s and 1930s, when the continent experienced hyperinflation. More recently, accountants in the United Kingdom and the United States have written some provocative essays about how to account for price-level changes.

Size and Complexity of Business Enterprises, Sophistication of Management and the Financial Community, and General Levels of Education

These factors define the limits of a country's accounting sophistication. Larger, more complex business enterprises have more difficult accounting problems. Highly trained accountants are needed to handle these more difficult problems; accounting cannot be highly developed in a country where general education levels are low, unless that country imports accounting talent or sends bright citizens elsewhere for the necessary training. At the same time, the users of a company's financial reports must themselves be sophisticated—or else there will be no demand for sophisticated accounting reports.

Most multinational corporations are headquartered in the wealthy, industrialized nations (e.g., Japan, Germany, Great Britain, and the United States). These countries have sophisticated accounting systems and highly qualified professional accountants. In contrast, education levels in most developing countries are low and businesses are small; as a result, accounting is primitive. From earlier discussions, however, it may occur to you that if accounting responds to information needs, then accounting in developing countries may very well be at an appropriate level of sophistication under the circumstances. While many accountants hold this view, some feel that the lack of sophisticated accounting ability in less developed countries actually impedes their potential for economic progress. It does appear, though, that newly developed countries (such as Taiwan, South Korea, and Brazil) have been able to overcome their rudimentary accounting expertise. And it is also true that developing accounting expertise has a high priority in many emerging market economies, for example, China, Poland, and the Czech Republic. Accounting development and economic development clearly go hand in hand.

Culture

The variables just enumerated are in varying degrees part of the culture of individual countries, races, religions, geographic areas, and other delineating features. Sometimes "culture" is defined as the collective programming of the human mind. In other words, it is the values and attitudes shared by members of society. So all the things we learn, observe, feel, believe, or prioritize have cultural dimensions. There is increasing attention in the accounting literature to cultural links as components of accounting concepts, standards, and practices. For example, it appears that individualistic cultures tend to have higher levels of accounting disclosure than group-oriented cultures. The latter tend to restrict the "need to know" to those within the group. Another cultural variable is whether society is comfortable with ambiguity and an uncertain future. Those that are not are termed "uncertainty avoidant." These societies seem to be cautious toward accounting measurements. That is, we find conservative measurement practices where uncertainty avoidance is strong.

It is imperative to recognize that accounting development is not random or arbitrary. Despite the difficulty of directly tying accounting development to cultural factors, many seasoned observers are convinced that such a link does exist. To quote one researcher: ". . . research has identified that environmental factors, especially cultural factors, exert considerable influence on a country's accounting practice development."[2] Exhibit 1–2 summarizes the environmental variables just discussed for nations with the six biggest economies in the world.

ACCOUNTING MODELS

The variables shaping the development of financial accounting overlap to some degree. For example, most code law countries have historically relied on either banks or the government to supply capital to businesses, whereas common law countries have historically relied on their more developed stock and bond markets to satisfy businesses' capital needs. Code law countries also tend to be uncertainty avoidant, whereas common law countries are much less so. If we

---

[2]Harry H. E. Fechner and Alan Kilgore, "The Influence of Cultural Factors on Accounting Practice," *International Journal of Accounting* 29, no. 3 (1994), p. 265.

EXHIBIT 1–2   Environmental Variables in Six Nations

Variable	United States	Japan	Germany	France	United Kingdom	Italy
External finance	Stock market	Banks	Banks	Banks; government	Stock market	Banks; government
Legal system	Common law	Code law	Code law	Code law	Common law	Code law
Political and economic ties	Canada, Japan, Mexico	U.S., Asia	Europe, U.S.	Europe	Europe, U.S., Commonwealth	Europe
Inflation	Low	Low	Low	Low	Low	Low
Complexity and sophistication; education	High	High	High	High	High	High
Culture						
• Individualism	High	Low	High	High	High	High
• Uncertainty avoidance	Weak	Strong	Strong	Strong	Weak	Strong

accept the idea that accounting is influenced by its environment, then it is logical to expect accounting similarities among countries with similar business environments.

Indeed, nations can be grouped or clustered according to accounting similarities. However, many of the national distinctions are getting blurred as capital becomes increasingly global and as more and more companies cross-list their shares on stock markets outside their home countries. It is also clear that the importance of stock markets as a source of external finance is growing around the world. Stock market development is a top priority of many countries, especially those emerging from centrally planned to market-oriented economies. Further, as discussed in Chapter 4, many companies now adopt *multiple* reporting approaches, whereby one set of financial statements complies with national requirements and another set complies with internationally accepted accounting standards. For example, the *annual report* of Roche, the large Swiss pharmaceutical company (www.roche.com), contains two sets of financial statements, one prepared according to International Accounting Standards (see Chapter 3) and another prepared according to Swiss company law. Therefore, rather than discussing accounting groupings on the basis of countries, your authors prefer to think of accounting "models" based on certain distinguishing features of accounting. National patterns that conform to these features are also identified.

The Fair Presentation/Full Disclosure Model

This model of accounting is oriented toward the decision needs of external investors. Financial statements enable investors to judge managerial performance and to predict future cash flows and profitability. Extensive disclosures provide additional relevant information for these purposes. Such financial statements are said to be a "fair" presentation of a company's financial position and results of operations.

The fair presentation/full disclosure model originated in Great Britain and spread around the world wherever British influence was felt, including the United States. As a result, this orientation of accounting is sometimes called *Anglo-Saxon* or *British-American*. It is found in common law countries, which, as noted above, also tend to rely on capital markets as the principal source of external finance for businesses. Australia, Canada, South Africa, and Singapore are other countries with this type of accounting.

The fair presentation/full disclosure model is also the approach adopted by the International Accounting Standards Committee, discussed in Chapter 3. It is particularly relevant for companies relying on international capital markets for finance. Many large French, German, and Swiss companies now prepare financial statements meant for their worldwide audience according to International Accounting Standards (IASs). (The example of Roche was noted previously. Parenthetically, some Japanese multinational companies have gravitated to U.S. accounting standards as a way to reach their investors around the world.) IASs are also the benchmark for some emerging market economies, such as China. Here the idea is to develop accounting that will attract external investors from other countries.

The Legal Compliance Model

The legal compliance model originated in the code law countries of Europe, such as France, Germany, and Italy. As a result, it is sometimes called the *Continental* model. Japan is also a code law country, having based its legal system on Germany's. Unlike the fair presentation/full disclosure model, this type of accounting is not designed to inform external investors. Instead, it is usually designed to satisfy such government-imposed requirements as computing income taxes or demonstrating compliance with the national government's macroeconomic plan. The income amount calculated can also be the basis for determining dividends to be paid to shareholders and bonuses to be paid to employees and managers. Conservative measurement practices ensure that such distributions from income are prudent. Income smoothing, discussed in the next chapter, is another common feature. Smooth patterns in income from year to year mean that tax, dividend, and bonus payouts are also more stable.

Banks are usually the important source of finance which, as discussed earlier, further encourages conservative measurement practices. Companies have close relationships not only with their banks, but also with their major customers and suppliers, and with labor. As "insiders," these groups are informed with private access to information. Consequently, the demand for public disclosure is low in the legal compliance model of accounting.

The Inflation-Adjusted Model

Price changes are a fact of life in most countries. How inflation affects accounting development was discussed above, and alternative accounting responses to inflation are covered in more detail in Chapter 2. Suffice it to say that when inflation is severe, accounting will incorporate inflation adjustments. The inflation-adjusted model may be viewed as something of an "add-on" to one of the two previous models. For example, accounting in Israel and Mexico shares most of the features of the fair presentation/full disclosure model, but with adjustments based on changes in the consumer price index. The countries of Central and South America got their accounting from code-law Europe. Except for the addition of accounting adjustments for inflation in certain of these countries, their accounting fits the description of the legal compliance model. Countries also abandon inflation adjustments once inflation is tamed. For example, this recently happened in Argentina and Brazil.

CONCLUSION

One should not say that the accounting in one country is of better quality than the accounting in another country. Accounting exists because it fulfills a need, and as long as accounting satisfies the needs of its user groups, it is doing what it is supposed to do. Accounting develops in and is nurtured by its environment. That the world is a potpourri of accounting practices reflects the diversity of uses to which it is put. At the same time, some of this diversity is fading. There is pressure for harmonizing accounting around the world in response to increasing economic interdependencies among nations and global capital flows.

APPENDIX

Accountants often classify countries by their type of accounting, and Exhibit 1–3 shows where certain countries have traditionally fit. However, as this chapter argues, national characteristics are becoming increasingly blurred. Accounting around the world is converging—at least to some extent—in response to mobile capital and the increasing global interdependencies of most economies. For the following reasons, we recommend a certain amount of caution when using this exhibit:

EXHIBIT 1–3   List of Selected Countries Comprising the Three Major Accounting
Models

Fair Presentation/Full Disclosure Model

Australia	Kenya	South Africa
Bangladesh	Malaysia	Taiwan
Canada	Netherlands	Thailand
Colombia	New Zealand	United Kingdom
Denmark	Nigeria	United States
India	Pakistan	Venezuela
Indonesia	Philippines	Zimbabwe
Ireland	Singapore	

Legal Compliance Model

Algeria	Germany	Portugal
Austria	Greece	South Korea
Belgium	Italy	Spain
Cameroon	Japan	Sweden
Cote d'Ivorie	Luxembourg	Switzerland
Egypt	Morocco	Turkey
Finland	Norway	Zaire
France		

Inflation-Adjusted Model

Argentina	Israel	Peru
Brazil	Mexico	Uruguay
Chile		

---

1. Some countries allow, or even require, companies to use different bases of accounting for their *consolidated* and their *unconsolidated* financial statements. The consolidated statements follow the fair presentation/full disclosure model, while the unconsolidated statements follow the legal compliance model. Examples are France, Germany, Italy, Japan, and Switzerland.[3]

2. One reason that some countries are not represented in the exhibit is that their economies are in transition from central planning to a market orientation. That means that their accounting is also in transition. Examples include China, the Czech Republic, Hungary, Poland, and Russia. Under central planning, the government owns the productive resources and supplies capital, and the

---

[3]Chapter 6 discusses consolidated financial statements. French, German, and Swiss companies are allowed to use International Accounting Standards in preparing their consolidated financial statements. Italian consolidated financial statements are also consistent with IASs. As the chapter notes, some Japanese companies use U.S. accounting standards in their consolidated financial statements. In all of these cases, however, unconsolidated financial statements still conform to local accounting standards.

primary users are government planners. Emphasis is on budgets and production quotas. *Managerial* accounting comes closer to describing the accounting scene than financial accounting. As these countries move sectors of their economies to a market orientation, they are typically adopting the fair presentation/full disclosure model as their benchmark. However, this overall accounting development is not yet far enough along to put them firmly in this group.

3. When inflation ebbs, countries opt out of the inflation-adjusted model. As noted in the chapter, Argentina and Brazil recently abandoned their inflation adjustments and Mexico intends to. However, if severe inflation returns, we may expect countries to re-opt for the inflation-adjusted model.

REVIEW QUESTIONS

1. Why is accounting shaped by the environment in which it operates?
2. Why is there diversity in financial accounting practices around the world?
3. List the variables that shape the development of accounting around the world and briefly discuss the influences of each.
4. What are the three major accounting models? What are the distinguishing characteristics of each?
5. Show how the variables listed in question 3 have affected each of the accounting models identified in question 4.
6. This chapter argues that many of the national distinctions of accounting are getting blurred. Why and in what ways is this happening?
7. The world's key political organizations (e.g., UN, OECD, IMF, EU, ASEAN) have operating units specifically concerned with international financial accounting standard setting and reporting. What is driving this international attention to accounting?

CASES

1–1 My Way or No Way

A leading U.S. accounting professor has been asked to deliver a lecture to some university students in Poland. The goal of his lecture is to impress upon the students that if they want to know how accounting ought to be done, they need look no further than the United States. The professor is impassioned about the quality of U.S. accounting. "It's simply the best," he says. He thought that before he discussed the quality of U.S. accounting with his Polish students, he would point out a few shortcomings that he sees with accounting in other countries. He is sketching out his notes and the following is what he has come up with so far:

- British accounting—too much wiggle room. "I appreciate the need for flexibility, but there's way too much latitude for judgment. As the old joke goes, 'Q: What's net income this year? A: What do you want it to be?'"
- German accounting—too conservative and too much income smoothing. "They undervalue assets and overvalue liabilities, and they use 'reserves' to shift income from one year to the next. How can you judge true performance this way?"
- Swiss accounting—too much secrecy/not enough disclosure. "Swiss accounting is like Swiss cheese. It's not so much what you see as what you don't see."
- Latin American accounting—inflation adjustments. "What the heck are these? Hey, if you just get rid of inflation, you don't have to worry about accounting for it."

Questions
1. What are possible explanations for the accounting practices that the professor has observed?
2. Do you agree with the professor that these observed practices are weaknesses of accounting in these countries?
3. What advice would you give the professor in preparing his lecture? Help him complete his thoughts.

1–2 Nifty NAFTA

Financial accounting and reporting practices in Canada, Mexico, and the United States have much in common. In all three countries, financial reporting focuses on investors and investor decision needs. However, there are some differences. Perhaps the two most important are (1) Mexico has inflation-adjusted accounting, while Canada and the United States practice historical cost accounting, and (2) there is less emphasis on full disclosure in Mexico than there is in Canada and the United States.

Questions
1. Why does accounting in Canada, Mexico, and the United States have much in common?
2. Explain the differences noted in the case.
3. What is the likely impact of the North American Free Trade Agreement (NAFTA) on financial accounting and reporting practices in Canada, Mexico, and the United States? Explain your reasoning.

EXHIBIT 1–4   Accounting Classification by Nair & Frank

Group I: *British* *Commonwealth*	*Group II:* *Latin* *American*	*Group III:* *Continental* *European*	*Group IV:* *United* *States*
Australia	Argentina	Belgium	Canada
Bahamas	Bolivia	France	Japan
Eire	Brazil	West Germany	Mexico
Fiji	Chile	Italy	Panama
Jamaica	Colombia	Spain	Philippines
Kenya	Ethiopia	Sweden	United States
Netherlands	India	Switzerland	
New Zealand	Paraguay	Venezuela	
Pakistan	Peru		
Rhodesia	Uruguay		
Singapore			
South Africa			
Trinidad & Tobago			
United Kingdom			

SOURCE: R. D. Nair and W. G. Frank, "The Impact of Measurement and Disclosure Practices on International Accounting Classifications," *The Accounting Review,* July 1980, p. 429.

1–3 Accounting Classifications—Who Cares?

Classifications exist in biology, political science, and law, to name but a few fields of study. Financial accounting systems have also been classified. The three "models" of accounting referred to in this chapter are one such classification. Exhibits 1–4, 1–5, and 1–6 are three others. Classifications are designed to highlight key characteristics that members of a group have in common and that distinguish various groups from each other. By pinpointing basic features that are similar within groups and different between groups, classifications help sharpen our overall understanding of whatever it is that is being classified.

Exhibit 1–4 is taken from a study by Nair and Frank. The authors relied on a database, developed by a large accounting firm, that contained the accounting practices in various nations. Statistical techniques were used to cluster 38 countries into the four groups shown in the exhibit.

Exhibit 1–5 was developed by Nobes, based on his understanding of accounting practices in 14 countries. Notice that it is hierarchical. In other words, one can tell not only which countries are in different categories but also how close or distant these categories are.

Exhibit 1–6 is a classification of accounting in 50 countries by Doupnik and Salter. They surveyed accountants in these countries to develop their database of accounting practices. Then they applied statistical methods to the data to get their

EXHIBIT 1–5 Accounting Classification by Nobes

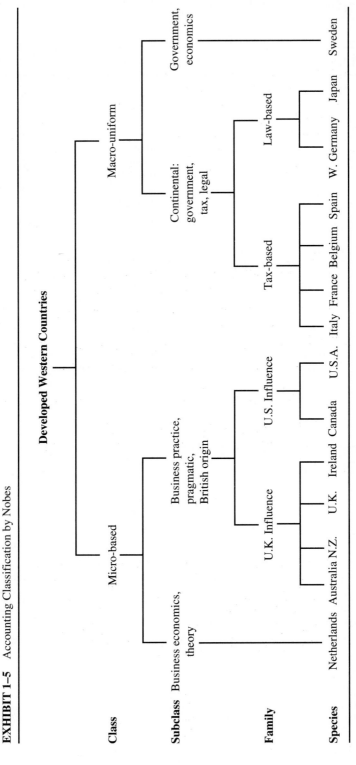

SOURCE: C. W. Nobes, "A Judgmental International Classification of Financial Reporting Practices," *Journal of Business Finance & Accounting*, Spring 1983, p. 7. Copyright held by Blackwell Publishers Ltd.

EXHIBIT 1–6 Accounting Classification by Doupnik & Salter

<table>
<tr><th rowspan="2">Country</th><th colspan="3">Number of Clusters</th></tr>
<tr><th>Two</th><th>Six</th><th>Nine</th></tr>
<tr><td>Japan</td><td rowspan="24">A2
Macro uniform</td><td>B6</td><td>C9</td></tr>
<tr><td>Germany</td><td>B5</td><td>C8</td></tr>
<tr><td>Finland</td><td rowspan="2">B4</td><td rowspan="2">C7</td></tr>
<tr><td>Sweden</td></tr>
<tr><td>Egypt</td><td rowspan="15">B3</td><td rowspan="7">C6</td></tr>
<tr><td>Saudi Arabia</td></tr>
<tr><td>Belgium</td></tr>
<tr><td>UAE</td></tr>
<tr><td>Liberia</td></tr>
<tr><td>Thailand</td></tr>
<tr><td>Panama</td></tr>
<tr><td>Portugal</td><td rowspan="8">C5</td></tr>
<tr><td>Spain</td></tr>
<tr><td>Colombia</td></tr>
<tr><td>Italy</td></tr>
<tr><td>Korea</td></tr>
<tr><td>Denmark</td></tr>
<tr><td>Norway</td></tr>
<tr><td>France</td></tr>
<tr><td>Argentina</td><td rowspan="5">B2</td><td rowspan="4">C4</td></tr>
<tr><td>Mexico</td></tr>
<tr><td>Brazil</td></tr>
<tr><td>Chile</td></tr>
<tr><td>Costa Rica</td><td>C3</td></tr>
<tr><td>Malaysia</td><td rowspan="26">A1
Micro based</td><td rowspan="26">B1</td><td rowspan="22">C2</td></tr>
<tr><td>S. Africa</td></tr>
<tr><td>Zimbabwe</td></tr>
<tr><td>Hong Kong</td></tr>
<tr><td>Singapore</td></tr>
<tr><td>Namibia</td></tr>
<tr><td>Ireland</td></tr>
<tr><td>United Kingdom</td></tr>
<tr><td>Zambia</td></tr>
<tr><td>Australia</td></tr>
<tr><td>Papua N. Guinea</td></tr>
<tr><td>New Zealand</td></tr>
<tr><td>Trinidad</td></tr>
<tr><td>Nigeria</td></tr>
<tr><td>Sri Lanka</td></tr>
<tr><td>Botswana</td></tr>
<tr><td>Jamaica</td></tr>
<tr><td>Philippines</td></tr>
<tr><td>Taiwan</td></tr>
<tr><td>Netherlands</td></tr>
<tr><td>Neth. Antilles</td></tr>
<tr><td>Luxembourg</td></tr>
<tr><td>Bermuda</td><td rowspan="4">C1</td></tr>
<tr><td>Israel</td></tr>
<tr><td>Canada</td></tr>
<tr><td>United States</td></tr>
</table>

SOURCE: T. S. Doupnik and S. B. Salter, "External Environment, Culture, and Accounting Practice," *International Journal of Accounting* 30, no. 3 (1995), p. 199.

classifications. Notice that, similar to Exhibit 1–5, there is a hierarchy in that they group countries into increasingly narrow clusters—the two-, six-, and nine-cluster groupings shown in the exhibit.

The three exhibits classify countries. They obviously differ in the number of countries classified, and they were done at different points in time. Nair and Frank use data on accounting practices from the early 1970s, Nobes' data are from the late 1970s, and Doupnik and Salter use accounting data as of 1990.

Questions
1. How do the three classifications by Nair and Frank, Nobes, and Doupnik and Salter compare and contrast? That is, what do they have in common and how do they differ?
2. What variables shaping accounting development would account for these classifications? What features of accounting would account for these classifications?
3. How do the classifications in these exhibits compare to the one in this chapter?
4. What practical benefits are there from studying classifications?

ADDITIONAL READINGS

Bailey, D. "Accounting in Transition in the Transitional Economy." *European Accounting Review* 4, no. 4 (1995), pp. 595–623. (Entire issue devoted to accounting in Eastern Europe and the former U.S.S.R.)

Chen, Y., P. Jubb, and A. Tran. "Problems of Accounting Reform in the People's Republic of China." *The International Journal of Accounting* 32, no. 2 (1997), pp. 139–53.

Davidson, R. A., A. M. G. Gerlardi, and F. Li. "Analysis of the Conceptual Framework of China's New Accounting System." *Accounting Horizons,* March 1996, pp. 58–74.

Doupnik, T. S., and S. B. Salter. "External Environment, Culture, and Accounting Practice: A Preliminary Test of a General Model of International Accounting Development." *The International Journal of Accounting* 30, no. 3 (1995), pp.189–207.

Eberhartinger, E. L. E. "The Impact of Tax Rules on Financial Reporting in Germany, France, and the U.K." *The International Journal of Accounting* 34, no. 1 (1999), pp. 93–119.

Gernon, H., and R. S. O. Wallace. "International Accounting Research: A Review of Its Ecology, Contending Theories and Methodology." *Journal of Accounting Literature* 14 (1995), pp. 54–106.

Nobes, C. "Towards a General Model of Reasons for International Differences in Financial Reporting." *Abacus,* September 1998, pp. 162–87.

Porcano, T. M., and A. V. Tran. "Relationship of Tax and Financial Accounting Rules in Anglo-Saxon Countries." *The International Journal of Accounting* 33, no. 4 (1998), pp. 433–54.

Salter, S. B. "Corporate Financial Disclosure in Emerging Markets: Does Economic Development Matter?" *The International Journal of Accounting* 33, no. 2 (1998), pp. 211–34.

Zeff, S. A. "A Perspective on the U.S. Public/Private-Sector Approach to the Regulation of Financial Reporting." *Accounting Horizons,* March 1995, pp. 52–70.

C H A P T E R

2

DIVERSITY IN FINANCIAL ACCOUNTING PRACTICES

LEARNING OBJECTIVES

1. Explain why and how financial accounting practice diversity is reduced within countries.
2. Understand why financial accounting practices differ between countries.
3. Describe several important areas of financial accounting diversity around the world.
4. Identify who wins and who loses as a result of worldwide accounting diversity.
5. Assess the likely consequences of worldwide accounting diversity.

In Chapter 1 we discussed the principal environmental variables that shape the development of national financial accounting systems. We identified:

1. External finance.
2. Legal system.
3. Political and economic ties with other countries.
4. Levels of inflation.
5. Size and complexity of business enterprises, sophistication of management and the financial community, and general levels of education.
6. Culture.

Chapter 3 is devoted to the idea of worldwide harmonization of the existing country-by-country financial accounting diversity. What is this diversity, and is it really problematic? Why is the enforcement of accounting rules and regulations a national activity? Who wins and who loses from national diversity in financial accounting practices? Questions such as these are explored in this chapter.

REDUCING DIVERSITY WITHIN COUNTRIES

Until the Great Depression of 1929 through 1930, companies everywhere could freely choose the accounting methods and rules they thought appropriate for their individual situations. In a 1972 book entitled *Main Street and Wall Street,* William Z. Ripley, then Harvard professor of political economy, described his review of U.S. corporate annual reports in these terms:

> Confronted with a great pile of recent corporate pamphlets on my table, the first impression is of their extraordinary diversity, in appearance, size, content, and intent. One premier concern, the Royal Baking Powder Company, fails to register any fiscal information at all, in as much as it has never issued a balance sheet or financial statement of any kind whatsoever for more than a quarter of a century . . . Akin to it is the Singer Manufacturing Company, which handles 80 percent of the world's output of sewing machines. Neither hide nor hair of financial data for this firm is discoverable in the usual sources of information. The dance-card, bald balance-sheet, or picture-book variety of corporation report follows hard upon these examples of complete reticence . . . Yet colored pictures of factories, brightly lighted at night,—as some of these must well have been in view of their extraordinary success,—tell no tales.[1]

Companies in the United States were incorporated under state law statutes, which generally contained only superficial accounting and financial reporting requirements. Code law countries had more elaborate corporate law provisions, but also literally nothing on accounting and financial reporting. This was a world of terrible misinformation and noncomparable financial statements. Essentially, corporate managements picked accounting and reporting rules that often pictured their companies financially better than they were in fact (this is called *window dressing* in accounting).

Remedies began to surface soon after the Great Depression. Countries subscribing to the fair presentation/full disclosure model of financial accounting created committees or boards of professional practicing accountants (certified public accountants [CPAs] in the United States; chartered accountants [CAs] in Canada and the United Kingdom) to recommend *generally accepted accounting principles* (GAAP) to be used within each country. In the United States, enforcement was assigned to the Securities and Exchange Commission (SEC), which is a federal government agency created to regulate all domestic markets for financial

---

[1]William Z. Ripley, *Main Street and Wall Street* (Houston, Tex.: Scholars Book Co., reprinted 1972), pp. 162–64.

EXHIBIT 2–1   Financial Accounting Standard Setting in Five Countries

Germany relies very heavily on legislation, particularly company law, and on taxation; accounting standards tend to be especially conservative and have very detailed provisions with respect to presentation and valuation. However, Germany recently established a private-sector body to determine accounting standards for consolidated financial statements.

France also depends on legal and tax decrees, although to a lesser degree than Germany. In 1998, a newly established government agency was assigned the responsibility of setting accounting standards.

Japan also draws heavily on legal and tax directives, so much so that the private sector has little direct involvement in setting accounting standards; in many ways, Japan's legal and tax systems follow those in Continental Europe.

In the **United Kingdom,** private-sector influence is very strong; standards tend to set out broad principles, with some latitude as to the details.

In the **United States,** the private sector is also the primary source of accounting standards, but with input and influence from the SEC; standard setting is a particularly lengthy process and, in addition to basic pronouncements, there is much detailed guidance.

SOURCE: International Capital Markets Group, *Harmonization of International Accounting Standards.* A paper prepared by the International Federation of Accountants with the assistance of Federation Internationale des Bourses de Valeurs and the International Bar Association Section on Business Law, 1992, p. vii. Updated by authors.

securities. Enforcement in the United Kingdom is more indirect in that it occurs mainly through litigation and other court processes. Countries subject to code laws (i.e., those following the legal compliance model) revised their respective companies' laws to require compliance with various accounting provisions and the orderly publication of financial statements.

Developing accounting and financial reporting methods and rules is called financial accounting *standard setting* (see Chapter 3). In some countries the *private sector* is mainly responsible for accounting standard setting, whereas in other countries, it is the *public sector.* Private sector groups include the accounting profession and other groups affected by financial reporting, such as users and preparers of accounting information. The public sector consists primarily of various government agencies, such as tax authorities and ministries responsible for commercial law.

As mentioned in Chapter 3, the Financial Accounting Standards Board (FASB), a private sector group, sets financial accounting standards in the United States. There were nearly 140 FASB standards at the end of 1999. Together with standards set before the FASB was established in 1973, these pronouncements constitute GAAP in the United States. However, other countries have different approaches to producing accounting standards. Exhibit 2–1 provides a comparative summary for five countries.

By and large, national accounting standard setters have been successful in reducing accounting and financial reporting diversity within their own country and they have forged clearly recognizable and nationally acknowledged country-by-country GAAP. The big concern now is that the GAAP of no two countries are the same. This means that financial information does not travel well internationally.

WHY FINANCIAL ACCOUNTING PRACTICES DIFFER BETWEEN COUNTRIES

Accounting and financial reporting are not the same everywhere. The three reasons discussed so far in this book are

1. Major environmental variables that shape accounting development in a country.
2. Adherence to a particular financial accounting model (by choice, affinity, or historical accident).
3. Process for setting national financial accounting standards.

There is a fourth critical factor that has to do with the very nature of accounting. This factor, conservatism, relates to all the uncertainties modern business must cope with. Here is how a group of experts describes what is going on:

> Financial statements, which are designed to portray the financial position and results of operations, are prepared at least annually. Businesses nowadays are involved in transactions which extend over significant time periods, and which have inherent uncertainties associated with them. As a result, at any accounting date there are often significant transactions which have not been completed, and where the final outcome is uncertain. This means that preparers of financial statements must make estimates about future events in order to apportion costs and revenues to the appropriate financial periods. Thus estimates have to be made about future costs and revenues on long-term contracts, on future pension costs, asset lives, and on many other matters. These are inherently difficult problems. There are not necessarily "right" answers, and it is therefore not surprising that countries deal with them in different ways.[2]

Conservatism, one of the cornerstones of financial accounting around the world, is one way to cope with these uncertainties. However, the extent to which conservatism affects accounting practices varies. As noted in Exhibit 2–1, for example, German accounting is especially conservative. U.K. accounting, on the other hand, is much less conservative.

Thus we have diversity from one set of GAAP to another among different countries. This diversity may well be justified in terms of one or a combination of the four reasons just mentioned, but the same diversity creates barriers for international financial information flows. It is one of the primary issues in international accounting.

---

[2]International Capital Markets Group, *Harmonization of International Accounting Standards.* A paper prepared by the International Federation of Accountants with the assistance of Federation Internationale des Bourses de Valeurs and the International Bar Association Section on Business Law, 1992, p. 3.

SOME EXISTING PRACTICE DIFFERENCES

When dealing with international accounting at a basic level, it is inappropriate to illustrate existing practice differences with elaborate examples. Therefore, *general* discussions of three topics follow the overview, which is presented first.

The subject matter of financial accounting divides itself into two dimensions—*measurement* and *disclosure.* Measurement concerns economic events and transactions whose effects are reflected directly on the three basic financial statements (i.e., the balance sheet, income statement, and cash flow statement). If an accounting entity borrows money from a bank, the amount of the debt is measured, and both the cash received and the debt payable are reflected on the next balance sheet and cash flow statement. Similarly, when a payroll comes due, all employee pay obligations are measured and social security/unemployment insurance/private pension contributions and other indirect employment costs are added to arrive at an appropriate amount for employment expenses on the next income statement. Measurement activities like these drive all formal accounting systems.

Aside from measurements themselves, readers of financial statements want to know which measurement methods were used and if there are items of interest that somehow could not be measured directly. Difficult-to-measure items include future effects of strikes, mergers, and product development. Also included are the benefits of investments in technology and human resources, environmental protection effects, or comparisons with another country's GAAP. These are often reported in supplemental disclosures, apart from the basic financial statements. Chapter 5 discusses disclosure issues. Accounting measurements are addressed in the rest of this chapter.

Assets and liabilities are often subject to significant measurement differences around the world. Take something as simple as cash. Most corporate balance sheets have a caption like "cash and cash equivalents." What does this cover? In the United States, demand deposits and highly liquid investments are included. In other countries, bank overdrafts and short-term borrowings are subtracted instead of being reported separately as liabilities.

Of course, there is the additional problem translating national currencies (see Chapter 6). Multinational corporations (MNCs) do business in many different countries and therefore have various bank accounts in as many countries. Companies like Kodak, Nestlé, or Procter & Gamble sell their products in more than 100 different countries and therefore have bank accounts in as many national currencies. To bring them all together into a single balance sheet requires *measuring* them in terms of a single currency. In other words, for Kodak all forms of cash equivalents must somehow be translated (i.e., remeasured) to U.S. dollars. What foreign exchange rate is appropriate for this purpose? Should one represent the resulting total as a U.S. dollar amount when, in fact, the majority of the funds involved is denominated in other national currencies?

If we have so much difficulty with a straightforward item like cash and cash equivalents, it is little wonder that even more substantive issues are encountered in relation to inventories, depreciable assets, intellectual properties, computer software, research and development, capitalized borrowing costs, leased proper-ties, intercorporate investments, and other assets.

The liabilities side of the accounting equation is equally complex. For decades, accountants have debated how to measure income tax accounting effects when financial accounting differs from tax accounting (i.e., within the fair pre-sentation/full disclosure model, since financial and tax accounting are highly sim-ilar in the legal compliance model). If a company takes relatively larger expense deductions for income tax purposes in connection with depreciation (and therefore postpones taxable income), should a *deferred income tax* effect be measured and put on the balance sheet? If the answer is yes, should it be measured using present value (i.e., discounted cash flow) methods? Is this item a liability like accounts or notes payable?

International liabilities measurement differences exist with respect to leasing contracts and contingencies like the eventual outcome of pending lawsuits. There is little international agreement on how to account for future contracts in the com-modities markets, interest rate swaps and similar arrangements in the financial markets, and hedging operations in the foreign exchange markets. Joint venture obligations are also a real measurement problem.

When it comes to measuring business net income or loss, things are still more complicated. The main sources of diversity in this area are

1. Avoidance of the income statement altogether: for example, taking unusual gains and losses, merger premium payouts, or certain financing transactions di-rectly to owners' equity on the balance sheet.

2. Creation of secret reserves in the name of prudence and conservatism in order to "manage" periodic business income reported to outsiders.

3. Impact of legal requirements that may necessitate setting up legal reserves to protect some tax advantages, treating executive bonuses and stock options on or off income statements, or dictating accruals by legal formula rather than economic effect.

In the preceding paragraphs, we have identified many accounting topics for which country-by-country measurement differences exist. International account-ing textbooks treat these differences in some detail. Many articles and mono-graphs present overviews of selected accounting issues where there is diversity in practice.

We now turn to three specific cases.

Goodwill

When a company buys another company, a business division, or some other business enterprise, it typically anticipates greater benefits than the fair market values of the net assets acquired. Maybe an added team of executives will bring about major synergy, maybe certain patents or processes lend themselves to higher profit potential, or maybe market access is at stake. Whatever the anticipated benefit, to the extent that purchase price exceeds total fair market value, something called *goodwill* is created (*negative goodwill* may occur in bargain purchases).

Considerable diversity exists among countries on whether purchased goodwill should be carried on balance sheets, and, if so, whether it should be amortized and how it should be amortized. Three main methods have emerged:

1. *Capitalization without amortization.* Under this method, goodwill is recognized as an asset with an indefinite life. Thus, it remains on the balance sheet.

2. *Capitalization with amortization.* Here goodwill is recognized as an asset with a finite life. It is written off over time either to income (which reduces annual income) or to equity (which does not reduce annual income). The shorter the life, the greater the write-off.

3. *Immediate write-off.* Instead of capitalizing, goodwill is written off at acquisition. Typically, it is written off to equity, which leaves annual income unaffected.

The goodwill accounting diversity is aggravated by a taxation effect. For instance, goodwill amortization is not tax deductible in the United Kingdom or the Netherlands, but it is deductible in Canada, Japan, Germany (post-1986), and the United States (post-1993). Obviously, the diversity involved affects business practices and therefore global competitiveness. If a company can permanently shield its income statements from goodwill amortization, it will report comparatively higher net earnings and thereby may gain a competitive advantage. Exhibit 2–2 summarizes goodwill accounting in selected countries.

Income Smoothing

Managers of most companies like to present a smooth income pattern from one year to the next, preferably a pattern with steady, predictable annual increases. A volatile income pattern normally suggests a company with higher risk of operations, which often leads to lower investor confidence and higher costs of obtaining financing. Smooth income normally means the opposite: less risk, greater investor confidence, and lower financing costs.

The opportunities allowed by GAAP to smooth income vary greatly around the world. The GAAP of some countries, for example, the United States, allow little flexibility for income smoothing. By contrast the practice is a notable feature of German and Swiss accounting. Here, GAAP have built-in flexibility that managers routinely take advantage of. The GAAP of still other countries actually encourage income smoothing by companies as a way to stimulate a long-term view of companies' operations and to encourage overall confidence in the nation's economy. Sweden is an example of such a country.

Of course, income smoothing can occur quite apart from anything permitted by a country's GAAP. This is because managers have discretion over the timing

EXHIBIT 2–2 Accounting for Goodwill in Selected Countries

	Capitalization and Amortization	Maximum Period of Amortization	Immediate Write-Off against Reserves	Tax Deductible
Australia	Required	20	No	No
Canada	Required	40*	No	Yes
France	Required	Not specified	No	No
Germany	Permitted	Not specified	Permitted	Yes
Japan	Required	5*	No	Yes
New Zealand	Required	20	No	No
United Kingdom	Required	20**	No	No
United States	Required	40*	No	Yes
International— Revised IAS 22	Required	20***	No	Not applicable

*A 20-year period is being considered.

**Twenty years is a rebuttable presumption. A longer life or an indefinite life (the latter resulting in no amortization) is possible if goodwill is subject to an annual impairment review.

***Longer periods can be justified if goodwill is subject to an impairment review.

SOURCE: M. C. Miller, "Goodwill Discontent: The Making of Australian and International Accounting Policy," *Australian Accounting Review*, June 1995, p. 8. Updated by authors.

of some revenue and expense transactions. For example, advertising costs can easily be shifted from one fiscal year to the next by merely accelerating or delaying expenditures by a week. Additional expenditures can be made just before year-end to reduce income; alternatively, they can be postponed to the first of the next year to increase income in the current year. In the overall scheme of things, such judicious timing of advertising transactions probably has little impact on the company, even in the short run. However, it obviously changes the amount of income reported in each of the two years, and correspondingly alters the year-to-year pattern.

The focus of this section, however, is on the quite legitimate use of accounting principles to shift income from one year to the next. In particular, this section discusses the use of *provisions* and *reserves* as income smoothing devices. While these two terms have other meanings in other accounting contexts, as used here, *provisions* refers to charges against income. They are a type of expense (or sometimes, loss) which normally requires judgment as to the amount. Obviously, there are many items like this, so there are potentially a number of provisions that a company may be dealing with. Examples include risks and uncertainties for product obsolescence and potential foreign exchange losses. Because judgment is involved, the amount of a provision is imprecise, and there is an inherent flexibility in its determination. In other words, a range of amounts is typically involved, and reasonable arguments can be made for any of the amounts within this range. This means that managers have discretion in choosing the amount of the provision that actually reduces income in any given year.

Reserves, as used here, refers to special equity accounts on the balance sheet used to accumulate the provisions taken over the years. When a provision is charged in the accounts, a corresponding amount is added to a reserve account. In other words, reducing income on the income statement by a provision amount means increasing a reserve account on the balance sheet by the same amount.

So how are provisions and reserves used to smooth income? One way is to judiciously choose the amounts of provisions that achieve the desired net income for the year. Or one might even omit a provision if "necessary" in some year. However, reserves can also be "drawn down" in particularly bad years to increase income. In other words, a reserve is decreased and a *negative* provision recorded in order to *increase* income.

A company may or may not disclose the activity in its provision and reserve accounts. If the amounts of provisions are combined with other expenses and if the amounts of reserves are combined with other stockholders' equity accounts, then a financial statement reader will not be able to tell the extent of their use or the impact on income. Sometimes people refer to this as using *secret* reserves. Alternatively, the effects of income smoothing may be fully revealed, allowing a financial statement reader to understand how income was affected by the use of provisions and reserves.[3]

Some observers argue that the use of provisions and reserves deceives financial statement readers. While this is arguably possible, it is important to bear in mind that, as discussed here, the practice is a legitimate application of a nation's GAAP, allowed or even encouraged in certain countries. Whether things are kept secret will also depend on what the country's GAAP require companies to reveal. In addition, income smoothing opportunities are often tied to a nation's income tax laws. In general, income smoothing is more often practiced in code law countries where financial and tax accounting are strongly linked. (See Chapter 1.) Finally, it was noted earlier in this chapter that there is diversity in how conservatism is interpreted and practiced around the world. All things being equal,

---

[3]A dramatic example of the use of reserves to smooth income was revealed by Daimler-Benz, the German automobile manufacturer of Mercedes-Benz, for its 1993 fiscal year. Daimler-Benz (now DaimlerChrysler) had recently listed its common stock shares on the New York Stock Exchange. One of the requirements imposed on non-U.S. companies listing their shares in the United States is that they reconcile their net income according to their home country's GAAP to net income according to U.S. GAAP. (In this way, non-U.S. companies reveal how the major GAAP differences between their home country and the United States affect reported income.) Under German GAAP, the 1993 net income of Daimler-Benz was DM615 million (DM = deutsche marks); however, under U.S. GAAP Daimler-Benz reported a net *loss* of DM1,839 million. The most important reason that the company went from a net income position under German GAAP to a net loss position under U.S. GAAP was the use of reserves. Daimler-Benz had drawn down its reserves accounts in 1993 to boost its German GAAP income. Using provisions and reserves to smooth income is not allowed under U.S. GAAP.

there will be a tendency to "overprovide" in countries where conservatism is particularly strong, compared to countries where conservatism is not so strong.

Asset Valuation

Financial accounting in most countries is based in part on the *historical cost principle.* This principle is based on the assumption that the currency unit used to report financial results is reasonably stable—that is, there is little or no inflation. As a result, strict historical cost accounting does not recognize the effects of inflation or other price changes. Keeping assets valued at their original transaction prices avoids having to make subjective determinations about how much more or less they are worth now compared to some earlier time. Accountants have traditionally believed that objective accounting information is more reliable than subjective information and, therefore, more useful.

However, as discussed in Chapter 1, severe inflation is a potent force that can strain the historical cost principle. Dramatic price changes make historical cost accounting information less believable and, therefore, less useful. The reasonableness of the historical cost principle varies inversely with the severity of price changes.

There are two basic approaches to accounting for changing prices. *General purchasing power (GPP) accounting* uniformly changes the values of assets and liabilities to reflect the general change in the currency unit's purchasing power. While transactions are initially recorded at their historical costs, they are later notched up or down by changes in the currency's general purchasing power. As a result, the items on the balance sheet and income statement are reported in units of the same purchasing power. *Current cost accounting* (CCA), on the other hand, changes the historical costs of assets to their current values and recognizes corresponding expenses at the current cost of obtaining the services represented by those expenses.

Only a very few countries *require* that the effects of changing prices be incorporated directly into the accounting records and financial statements. This points out that while inflation can put a severe strain on the historical cost model of accounting, historical cost nevertheless has a strong hold on accounting practices. Historical cost is still the predominant basis for preparing financial statements. The GAAP of some countries, though, allow companies to reflect the effects of changing prices if they choose to do so. And the GAAP of still other countries suggest that the impacts of fluctuating prices be disclosed supplementally—apart from the main financial statements.

The International Accounting Standards Committee (IASC) recommends in *Standard 29,* "Financial Reporting in Hyperinflationary Economies," that when a company is reporting in the currency of a country experiencing very high levels of inflation, the financial statements should be restated to reflect the purchasing power of that currency unit at year-end. In other words, *Standard 29* requires comprehensive GPP accounting for a company reporting in the currency of a "hyperinflationary" economy.

General Purchasing Power Accounting.   The inflation-adjusted model of accounting was discussed in Chapter 1. It is most often associated with Latin America. These countries have contended with high inflation rates for a long time and, as a result, accounting for changing prices is an issue too serious for their accountants to ignore. Bolivia, Chile, and Mexico require companies to comprehensively restate their financial statements on the basis of changes in general purchasing power. Several others require that fixed assets be revalued at certain intervals for changes in the price level. (Since fixed assets are not replaced as often as current assets, their historical costs are more likely to be out of date with persistently high price changes.) Depreciation expense is calculated on the restated values of fixed assets. A few other Latin American countries also accept such restatements.

Current Cost Accounting.   Many accountants automatically think of the Netherlands when CCA is mentioned. That is because Dutch accountants have devoted more attention to it over longer periods of time than accountants in other countries. The Dutch professor Theodore Limperg (1879–1961) is often called the father of *replacement value theory,* from which current cost accounting is derived. Accounting in the Netherlands is heavily influenced by business economics (or *microeconomics*). A fundamental notion in business economics is that the input values of a company's goods and services must be less than their selling prices in order to maintain long-run profitability and, hence, ensure survival. Use of current values is thought to best accomplish this, while at the same time preserving the amounts permanently invested in the business firm.

Piecemeal Approaches.   Many countries allow the selective use of CCA. This means that only some assets (e.g., fixed assets that are depreciated or property held for investment purposes) are revalued to current market values and that such revaluations are done at management's discretion. Thus, financial statement readers must be careful to both understand a company's accounting policies and carefully read its footnote disclosures.

Exhibit 2–3 summarizes asset valuation in selected countries.

CONSEQUENCES OF WORLDWIDE ACCOUNTING DIVERSITY

Enough evidence is available to conclude resolutely that GAAP differ (at times substantially) from country to country. Whether this is good or bad depends on the points of view of a variety of interest groups.

Corporate Management

Managers of companies with strictly domestic operations care little. As long as national GAAP are relatively clear, useful, and broadly applied, most medium-

EXHIBIT 2–3   Selected Country Practices for Asset Revaluation

Country	Revaluations of PP&E
IAS (includes China, Switzerland, approx. 20 others)	Allowed but then must be kept current using professional evaluation.
United States	Not allowed.
United Kingdom	Allowed with broad discretion; current proposal would narrow choices but still allow revaluation. Investment properties must be fair-valued annually.
France	Allowed but rare, occasionally required by law.
Germany	Not allowed.
Netherlands	Allowed and usually updated annually.
Italy	Allowed but rare, occasionally required by law.
Japan	Not allowed.
Brazil	Traditionally part of inflation accounting, which varies with law being applied.
Mexico	Required as part of inflation-accounting system.

SOURCE: T. S. Harris, *Apples to Apples: Accounting for Value in World Markets* (New York: Morgan Stanley Dean Witter, 1998), p. 5.

sized and small companies feel well served by the accounting rules they have to contend with. In this regard, there are no problems.

MNCs see it differently. They face global competition every day and sense that accounting diversity affects competitiveness. If a European corporation can bid for a U.S. acquisition target company and immediately write off all premium payouts to owners' equity (bypassing the income statement), it might outbid an equally interested U.S. corporation that must amortize the same premium payouts as goodwill through subsequent income statements. MNCs like "level playing fields" for their global operations. Distorting factors cause barriers and retaliation.

Companies are also increasingly listing their common stock shares on foreign stock markets. They do so mainly to reduce their cost of capital: by tapping capital from around the world, they expand the availability of investment funds and broaden their shareholder base. Some companies also like to list their shares in countries where they have operations (especially manufacturing facilities). This helps build ties and enhances name recognition in that country. Yet the advantages of multiple stock exchange listings come at a cost. Working with many different national GAAP requirements is an expensive proposition. Moreover, companies must be careful to communicate effectively with their foreign shareholders, a topic explored in Chapter 4.

Investors

Portfolio investors and their agents, financial analysts, probably dislike international accounting diversity the most. Instant global communications and overall cheap and quick access to global financial markets have made cross-border investing very attractive. Since national business cycles are not synchronized around the world, advantages are available from judicious diversification of investments involving different national securities markets. Financial misinformation short-circuits this process.

Investors experience frustrations when they do not understand whether financial statements merely look similar or are in fact similarly prepared. Underwriters consistently report that worldwide accounting diversity causes some underwriting (i.e., pricing of new securities issues) difficulties. If investors, analysts, and underwriters indeed experience difficulties with GAAP diversity, financial markets are not as efficient as they could be and therefore returns to investors are less than they ought to be. This is a powerful indictment of GAAP diversity.

Stock Markets and Regulators

Stock markets and regulators have twin goals of *investor protection* and *market quality*. To protect investors, most stock markets (along with professional or governmental regulatory agencies) require listed companies to disclose sufficient information so that investors can assess their past performance and future prospects. Investors are also protected by enforcing disclosure requirements. In other words, investor protection is accomplished by adequate and credible accounting and other disclosures. Market quality is achieved by fair and efficient trading and by the availability of investment opportunities for market participants.

Stock markets and regulators interpret these goals differently around the world. For example, accounting and disclosure requirements for listing shares vary extensively. Research shows that MNCs consider these requirements to be an important cost when they choose where to list their common stock shares. Indeed, MNCs are less likely to choose stock exchanges that require them to make extensive new disclosures over and above those that they are already making at home.

The United States has the most extensive accounting and disclosure requirements in the world. The U.S. Securities and Exchange Commission (SEC) is the regulatory agency responsible for these requirements. In general, the SEC believes that investors are better protected when there is a "level playing field," that is, when comparable accounting information is provided by U.S. and non-U.S. companies alike. Nevertheless, non-U.S. companies allege that they avoid listing in the United States because they find U.S. requirements too onerous. If this is true, then U.S. citizens are deprived easy access to buying shares in these companies, and the U.S. capital market may become less competitive globally. The situation shows how the twin goals of investor protection and market quality can conflict. It represents a vexing problem for the SEC that it has yet to resolve.

Accounting Professionals and Standard Setters

Some have suggested that accounting professionals, especially those in the Big Five professional firms, like diversity because it generates fees for them all the way from assisting in setting up new business units for their clients in different GAAP territories to restating financial reports from one set of GAAP to another (see Chapter 4). GAAP diversity also makes cross-border auditing more costly and therefore raises auditing fees. Even though not demonstrated by reliable research, it stands to reason that at least some accounting professionals gain from the GAAP diversity factor.

Accounting standard setters, as guardians of the public interest, would like to have full authority over all GAAP and financial reporting of companies whose securities are publicly held or whose size is so large that the public interest is affected. But regulations are primarily enforced through national laws and national legal systems. Therefore, a national focus is inevitable for accounting regulation—at least for the time being. Moreover, national regulators want discretion over national GAAP. International or any other GAAP are beyond their reach of influence and hence unacceptable. Nationalism is an issue here. Do you want others (i.e., non-nationals) to have determining influence over the GAAP you are required to use? Many countervailing forces come to bear on this point.

CONCLUSION

Worldwide diversity in financial accounting and reporting exists. Four specific reasons explain this diversity. In some instances, the diversity among national GAAP is significant; in others it is not. There are some winners and some losers as a result of the diversity condition. When diversity reaches the point of misinformation, it becomes dysfunctional. National environmental factors together with national laws and national accounting standard setting systems will make some degree of GAAP diversity inevitable. However, in domestic terms, national GAAP have reduced practice diversity. A similar degree of diversity reduction may be desirable on the international level. Harmonization of accounting practices is aimed at such reduction and is explored in Chapter 3.

REVIEW QUESTIONS

1. Are within-country accounting practices more or less diverse than cross-country practices? Explain.
2. Explain the effect(s) of national financial accounting standard setting on international practice diversity.
3. List the four reasons identified in this chapter that cause international accounting practice diversity. Which one do you consider most important? Why?

4. Why is accounting for purchased goodwill a controversial international accounting issue?

5. Explain how companies from certain countries use provisions and reserves to smooth income. Is income smoothing good or bad? Why?

6. What are the three basic approaches for valuing assets? Where and under what circumstances is each one observed in practice?

7. Who wins and who loses from worldwide diversity in financial accounting and reporting practices? Present reasoned answers in no more than four short paragraphs.

CASES

2–1 The Goodwill Bugbear

Quotient Enterprises acquired the assets of Limited Company during the current financial year. The acquired assets had a fair market value of $222 and were purchased for $1,050. At the end of the current financial year, Quotient's consolidated total assets (including the $222, but not goodwill) amounted to $2,779; stockholders' equity was $1,958. Consolidated income for the current financial year (ignoring any potential goodwill amortization) is $361.

Quotient's accountants are preparing the financial statements for the current financial year and wish to know how alternative ways to account for goodwill potentially affect the income statement and balance sheet. Management is concerned with how certain financial ratios will "look" to investors and financial analysts under the alternatives.

Questions
1. What are the different internationally permitted methods of accounting for goodwill, including permitted amortization periods?

2. What are the amounts of total assets and stockholders' equity under each permitted alternative? What are the income amounts under each permitted alternative?

3. Under each alternative, what are the ratios of (a) net income to total assets and (b) net income to stockholders' equity?

4. Does the international diversity in accounting for goodwill affect a company's relative competitive advantage in making business acquisitions? Explain.

2–2 Home Country Accounting Isn't Always Good Enough

National stock market regulatory agencies around the world share similar goals, including the following: (1) protecting investors by ensuring adequate financial and other information disclosures, (2) keeping the nation's stock market(s) competitive on a global basis, (3) promoting the availability of investment opportunities for the nation's citizens, and (4) safeguarding the fairness, efficiency, and stability of the nation's stock market(s). The U.S. Securities and Exchange Commission (SEC) is the agency responsible for regulating stock markets in the United States.

U.S. companies face the most extensive accounting and disclosure requirements of any companies in the world. In general, the SEC requires non-U.S. companies wishing to have their shares traded on U.S. stock exchanges to present equivalent information to that by U.S. companies. International accounting diversity presents a particular problem for the SEC. "Leveling the playing field" by requiring additional information from non-U.S. companies treats all MNCs alike and provides investors with comparable information for their decision making. Yet many observers allege that non-U.S. companies are avoiding U.S. capital markets because SEC requirements are so much more extensive than those elsewhere around the world.

Arthur Levitt, Chairman of the SEC, made the following comments in a speech at the AICPA's 26th Annual National Conference on Current SEC Developments (December 1998):

> We are very sensitive to the costs associated with non-uniform standards—particularly those relating to accounting. But as we attempt to answer the call for more harmony, we must focus, first and foremost, on the needs of capital markets and capital market participants.
>
> Participation in U.S. capital markets delivers great benefits—but membership has a price. While we are looking for ways to reduce costs, we will not do so by diminishing the benefits our markets provide.
>
> I don't presume to demand that the world's capital markets adopt our standards. But, any set of global accounting standards must satisfy a fundamental test—does it provide the necessary transparency, comparability, and full disclosure?[4]

Questions

1. What conflicts are inherent in the goals, identified above, of national stock market regulatory agencies?

2. Should the SEC "level the playing field" by requiring non-U.S. companies to provide information equivalent to that provided by U.S. companies? Who wins and who loses in this scenario?

3. Should the SEC allow an "unlevel playing field" by accepting less financial accounting information from non-U.S. companies than it requires from U.S. companies? Who wins and who loses in this scenario?

4. How would elimination of existing international accounting diversity simplify the lives of SEC commissioners?

---

[4]*IASC Insight,* March 1999, p. 5.

2–3 You Smooth You Lose

Consider the following comments by Louis Lowenstein, Professor Emeritus of Finance & Law at Columbia University. They are taken from his article, "Financial Transparency and Corporate Governance: You Manage What You Measure," *Columbia Law Review,* June 1996, pp. 1335–62. (Reprinted by permission.)

> [E]xecutives routinely manage today what they know *we* [accountants] will measure tomorrow. (p. 1336)
>
> [L]ook at the undesignated, hidden reserves used by German corporations and others . . . Europeans like to say that these provisions or reserves are prudent or conservative, but look at the effects. Clarity and consistency of disclosure suffer; one company's earnings cease to be comparable with another's. And those reserves, which do "conservatively" understate earnings when they are created, will overstate earnings or hide losses when reversed. Daimler-Benz reversed provisions and reserves totaling DM1.8 billion in the first half of 1993, creating a German-style "profit" at a time when its operations experienced a reality-style loss. (p. 1341)
>
> [C]onservative becomes a code word for concealment, as if disclosure were somehow the enemy of prudence. In practice, management behind a veil becomes management without accountability, and what eventually emerges may look less prudent than pungent. (p. 1358)

Questions

1. Professor Lowenstein argues that "you manage what you measure." What does he mean? [Hint: You may wish to read Professor Lowenstein's article.]

2. Does the use of secret provisions and reserves allow managers to hide losses? Why or why not?

3. Some people argue that income smoothing allows managers to maintain a long-run strategic focus in operating a company because they do not have to worry about how investors react to short-run fluctuations in profits. Do you agree? Why or why not?

4. Is income smoothing bad? Why or why not?

ADDITIONAL READINGS

Alexander, D., and S. Archer. *European Accounting Guide,* 3rd ed. San Diego: Harcourt Brace, 1998, 1,500 pp.

Doupnik, T. S., E. Martins, and G. Barbieri. "Innovations in Brazilian Inflation Accounting." *International Journal of Accounting* 30, no. 4 (1995), pp. 302–17.

Frost, C. A., and M. H. Lang. "Foreign Companies and U.S. Securities Markets: Financial Reporting Policy Issues and Suggestions for Future Research." *Accounting Horizons,* March 1996, pp. 95–109.

Haller, A. "Comparative Analysis of Major Accounting Issues." Chapter 16 in *International Accounting,* eds. P. Walton, A. Haller, and B. Raffournier (London: International Thompson Business Press, 1998), pp. 324–35.

Hanks, S. "Foreign Company Listings in the United States." *International Journal of Accounting* 34, no. 1 (1999), pp. 1–10.

Harris, T. S. *Apples to Apples: Accounting for Value in World Markets.* New York: Morgan Stanley Dean Witter, 1998, 20 pp.

Johnson, L. T., and K. R. Petrone. "Is Goodwill an Asset?" *Accounting Horizons,* September 1998, pp. 293–303.

Jones, M., and H. Mellett. "An International Bugbear." *Accountancy International,* May 1999, pp. 76–77.

Tweedie, D., and G. Whittington. "The End of the Current Cost Revolution." In *The Development of Accounting in an International Context: A Festschrift in Honour of R. H. Parker*, eds. T. E. Cooke and C. W. Nobes (London: Routledge, 1997), pp. 149–76.

Zeff, S. A. "Sitting on the Fence." *Accountancy International,* July 1999, pp. 68–69.

C H A P T E R

3

HARMONIZATION OF FINANCIAL ACCOUNTING DIVERSITY

LEARNING OBJECTIVES

1. Understand the purposes of accounting and auditing standards and how they are related.

2. Become familiar with some pros and cons of setting and applying international accounting and auditing standards.

3. Learn how the International Accounting Standards Committee (IASC) and International Federation of Accountants (IFAC) are harmonizing accounting and auditing standards.

4. Learn about the roles played by the European Union (EU), Organization for Economic Cooperation and Development (OECD), and United Nations (UN) in international accounting harmonization.

5. Assess the future direction of accounting and auditing harmonization internationally.

Chapter 1 explains how certain environmental variables shape the development of accounting in a particular country. It also provides a rationale for the worldwide diversity of accounting practices—since accounting reflects the environment in which it operates and since environments differ around the world, it follows that accounting will also be different around the world. The worldwide diversity in financial accounting practices is addressed in Chapter 2.

EXHIBIT 3–1   Websites of Organizations Mentioned in Chapter 3

Organization	*Website Address*
Accounting Standards Board (Australia)	*www.aarf.asn.au*
Accounting Standards Board (U.K.)	*www.asb.org.uk*
Canadian Institute of Chartered Accounts	*www.cica.ca*
European Union	*europa.eu.int*
Financial Accounting Standards Board	*www.fasb.org*
International Accounting Standards Committee	*www.iasc.org.uk*
International Federation of Accountants	*www.ifac.org*
International Organization of Securities Commissions	*www2.iosco.org*
Organization for Economic Cooperation and Development	*www.oecd.org*
United Nations	*www.unsystem.org*

Accounting and auditing standards play key roles in financial reporting. One way to reduce diversity (i.e., bring harmony) is to set and then enforce common standards for all concerned. This is what Chapter 3 is about. Exhibit 3–1 lists the websites of the organizations discussed in this chapter.

ACCOUNTING AND AUDITING STANDARDS

Accounting standards are the rules for preparing financial statements: that is, the "generally accepted accounting principles" (GAAP) that specify the type of information that financial statements ought to contain and how that information ought to be prepared. Accounting standards define what are acceptable and unacceptable financial accounting practices.

Auditing standards are the rules governing how an *audit* is performed. An audit of financial statements is the technical process by which an independent person (the auditor) gathers evidence to form an opinion about how well a set of financial statements conforms to GAAP. In most countries, a particular group of accountants is legally sanctioned to conduct financial statements audits. In the United States, for example, it is the certified public accountant (CPA). In the United Kingdom, it is the chartered accountant; in the Netherlands, the register accountant; and in Germany, the Wirtschaftsprüfer. Financial statements conforming to GAAP are said to be "reliable," and reliable information is an important ingredient in good decision making.

Accounting standards and auditing standards are interrelated. Accounting standards presumably define what is *useful* financial information. Auditing standards guide an auditor in determining whether it is also *reliable*. Useful and reliable financial information puts investors, creditors, and others in a position to make better decisions.

Accounting has been called the language of business. That analogy is accurate, since accounting is a form of communication. As with all types of communication, though, misunderstandings can arise unless meanings are reasonably clear.

To minimize the possibility of misunderstood financial communications, approximately 50 countries have created their own national financial accounting standard setting mechanisms. This has harmonized financial accounting diversity *within* countries. Unfortunately, international diversity continues to exist. This diversity results in a general lack of comparability in financial reports from one country to the next. As a result, there is a risk of misunderstanding when financial statements are communicated transnationally. The ensuing problems for users and preparers of financial reports are outlined in Chapter 4.

The problem of different auditing standards is more subtle. Fundamentally, an audit assures users that they can trust the information communicated by the financial statements. However, if auditors around the world are not comparably trained or if they do not observe comparable standards, then their work varies in quality. As a result, the inherent reliability of financial statements also varies.

PROS AND CONS OF INTERNATIONAL ACCOUNTING AND AUDITING STANDARDS

Every international accounting textbook and many international accounting research studies contain long lists of benefits and costs arising from international accounting and auditing standard setting. Among the alleged benefits, these sources mention greater international comparability of financial reports most often. Financial executives think that a more level playing field will result if international accounting standards are widely used—with reference to items such as cross-border mergers and acquisitions, and securing financing outside the home country. Some economists believe that such standards would improve global business competition, and some international agencies (e.g., UN) advocate international standards as a form of assistance to developing countries. In a more operational sense, international standards may reduce bookkeeping costs and allow more efficient preparation of financial statements.

Researchers have identified still other benefits: for example, reconciliation of sometimes adversarial interests between preparers and users of financial statements. Standardization is thought to bring more efficiency to analysis and use of financial reports and, pointedly, increase the credibility of the entire financial reporting system.

Of course, there are also those who object to the very idea of international accounting and auditing standards. In the early 1970s, critics condemned international standard setting as a solution too simple for a problem too complex. Other challenges point to inherent differences in national backgrounds and traditions, the potential breach of national sovereignty, politicalization of the entire field of accounting, plus standards overload if both national and international standards have to be applied concurrently. Some even question the need for international standards.

Nevertheless, the movement toward international standards for accounting and auditing is growing. By the late 1990s, critics were in the clear minority. The debate turned from whether we should have international standards to what is the best way to achieve them.

MAJOR ORGANIZATIONS PROMOTING INTERNATIONAL ACCOUNTING HARMONIZATION

We now turn our attention to the key players involved in harmonizing accounting and auditing standards around the world.

International Accounting Standards Committee

The *International Accounting Standards Committee* (IASC) was formed in 1973 by an agreement of the leading professional accounting bodies in Australia, Canada, France, Germany, Japan, Mexico, the Netherlands, the United Kingdom, Ireland, and the United States. It now represents more than 130 accountancy bodies from over 100 countries, which are listed in Exhibit 3–2.

The objectives of the IASC as set out in its constitution are:

1. To formulate and publish in the public interest accounting standards to be observed in the presentation of financial statements and to promote their worldwide acceptance and observance.

2. To work generally for the improvement and harmonization of regulations, accounting standards, and procedures relating to the presentation of financial statements.

To date, the IASC has issued 39 *International Accounting Standards* (IASs), four of which have been superceded. Those mentioned elsewhere in this text are

Standard 14, "Segment Reporting."

Standard 15, "Information for Reflecting the Effects of Changing Prices."

Standard 21, "The Effects of Changes in Foreign Exchange Rates."

Standard 27, "Consolidated Financial Statements and Accounting for Investments in Subsidiaries."

Standard 29, "Financial Reporting in Hyperinflationary Economies."

The International Accounting Standards Committee is governed by a Board consisting of representatives from up to 13 countries, including the founding member countries listed earlier and four organizational members.[1] Before approving a *Standard,* the board exposes it for public comment and seeks input from all IASC member bodies. The board meets several times a year in a different city in order to secure a variety of viewpoints. For example, meetings were recently

---

[1]At the time of writing, the Board had proposed a restructuring. The reader should consult the IASC's web site (www.iasc.org.uk) for the latest information on its structure.

EXHIBIT 3–2   Professional Accountancy Bodies in the Following Countries Are Members of IASC

Argentina	Honduras	Panama
Australia	Hong Kong	Paraguay
Austria	Hungary	Peru
Bahamas	Iceland	Philippines
Bahrain	India	Poland
Bangladesh	Indonesia	Portugal
Barbados	Iran	Romania
Belgium	Ireland	Saudi Arabia
Bolivia	Israel	Sierra Leone
Botswana	Italy	Singapore
Brazil	Ivory Coast	Slovenia
Bulgaria	Jamaica	South Africa
Cameroon	Japan	Spain
Canada	Jordan	Sri Lanka
Chile	Kenya	Sudan
China	Korea	Swaziland
Colombia	Kuwait	Sweden
Costa Rica	Lebanon	Switzerland
Croatia	Lesotho	Syria
Cyprus	Liberia	Taiwan
Czech Republic	Libya	Tanzania
Denmark	Luxembourg	Thailand
Dominican Republic	Madagascar	Trinidad and Tobago
Ecuador	Malawi	Tunisia
Egypt	Malaysia	Turkey
El Salvador	Malta	Uganda
Fiji	Mexico	United Kingdom
Finland	Namibia	United States of America
France	Netherlands	Uruguay
Germany	New Zealand	Venezuela
Ghana	Nicaragua	Vietnam
Greece	Nigeria	Yugoslavia
Guatemala	Norway	Zambia
Haiti	Pakistan	Zimbabwe

SOURCE: IFAC Web page: www.ifac.org, September 27, 1999.

held in Venice, Amsterdam, and Sao Palo. IASC board meetings are open to public observation.

During the initial phase of its life (from 1973 until the late 1980s), the IASC issued rather broad standards that normally allowed several alternative measurement options and prescribed only minimal disclosures. Accounting treatments accepted in the United Kingdom and the United States were always included in

IASs. Facing criticism for the "free choices" allowed in most IASs, in 1989 the IASC published *Exposure Draft 32 (E32)*, "Comparability of Financial Statements." The launch of the "Comparability/Improvements Project" (as it came to be called) was the IASC's most ambitious project to date. It aimed at eliminating most of the choices between various alternative accounting methods allowed under former IASs.

At this time, the IASC also began cooperating closely with the International Organization of Securities Commissions (IOSCO). IOSCO is a federation of securities markets regulators from over 80 countries. (The SEC is the U.S. member.) IOSCO is concerned with a broad array of regulatory issues brought on by the globalization of the world's capital markets. Such issues include international mergers and acquisitions, insider trading and market manipulation, and accounting and auditing standards for the purpose of securities listings. The concern is that there be comparable regulatory oversight among the world's securities markets. Even before the publication of *E32,* IOSCO had encouraged the IASC to eliminate accounting alternatives in existing IASs, to make them more detailed and complete, and to include adequate disclosure requirements. Thus, by enlisting IOSCO's cooperation, the IASC hoped to get IASs accepted for use on the world's capital markets. IOSCO's endorsement of IASs is necessary if this is to happen.

The IASC completed the Comparability/Improvements Project in 1993, but rather than endorsing them, IOSCO presented additional issues that it felt needed to be addressed. Altogether, IOSCO specified 24 "core" standards to be completed before it would consider endorsing (and promoting) IASs for cross-border listings of securities on the world's stock markets. Thus, the Comparability/Improvements Project evolved into the "core standards project," which the IASC completed in December 1998. Many observers feel that IOSCO endorsement is contingent on whether the U.S. SEC accepts IASs for non-U.S. listed companies. At the time of writing, the outcome of this scenario is highly uncertain.

In 1993, the IASC started collaborating with four "Anglo-American" accounting standard setting bodies, specifically, the Australian Accounting Standards Board, the Canadian Accounting Standards Board, the U.K. Accounting Standards Board, and the U.S. Financial Accounting Standards Board. Collectively, the group became known as the G4+1. (New Zealand began participating later.) Recall from Chapter 1 that, like IASs, all of these countries adhere to the "fair presentation/full disclosure" model of accounting. Given their shared aims, it seemed likely that cooperation would result in common solutions to accounting issues and thus promote international harmonization. Among the issues that have been considered are reporting financial performance, accounting for business combinations, and accounting for financial instruments. Activities of the G4+1 bodes well for closer coordination among national accounting standard setters and between standard setters and the IASC.

In your authors' opinion, support for the IASC and recognition of its *Standards* are growing around the world. The IASC is increasingly viewed as an effective voice for defining acceptable "world class" accounting principles. For example, hundreds of companies (mainly large MNCs and international financial institutions) state that they prepare their financial reports in accordance with IASs. Many countries use IASs as the basis for their own national accounting standards, and many stock exchanges accept IAS financial statements for cross-border listing purposes. Of course, as discussed above, the United States is a notable exception to the latter. Still, the U.S. SEC does allow foreign companies with shares traded in the United States to present cash flow statements in conformity with IAS 7 (*Cash Flow Statements*). It accepts IASC treatment of goodwill amortization, business acquisitions, and translation of the financial statements of subsidiaries operating in hyperinflationary economies—all for registrants who are foreign companies.

International Federation of Accountants

The *International Federation of Accountants* (IFAC) was formed in 1977 to develop a worldwide accountancy profession. Thus, it is mainly concerned with professional accountants rather than accounting principles. Its members are drawn from 143 professional accounting bodies in 104 countries, representing over 2 million accountants. Exhibit 3–3 shows IFAC's mission statement and the related action goals.

IFAC's International Auditing Practices Committee issues *International Standards on Auditing* (ISAs), designed to harmonize the way audits are con-

---

EXHIBIT 3–3   IFAC's Mission Statement

The International Federation of Accountants (IFAC) is the worldwide organization for the accountancy profession. The mission of IFAC is the development and enhancement of the profession to enable it to provide the public interest with services of consistently high quality.

To achieve this goal, IFAC will pursue the following objectives:

- Enhance the standards and development of the profession by issuing technical and professional guidance and by promoting the adoption of IFAC and IASC pronouncements.

- Promote the profession's role, responsibilities, and achievements in advancing the interest of member bodies and in serving the public interest.

- Foster a strong and cohesive profession by providing leadership on emerging issues, coordinating with regional organizations and member bodies and assisting them to achieve strategic objectives.

- Assist with the formation and development of national and regional organizations that serve the interests of accountants in public practice, commerce, industry, public sector, and education.

- Liaise with international organizations to influence the development of efficient capital markets and international trade in services.

SOURCE: IFAC, *Annual Report 1998*.

ducted worldwide. There are ISAs on such topics as the objectives and principles governing an audit, audit planning, evaluating internal controls, and gathering audit evidence. Its Education Committee works toward harmonizing the qualifications for becoming a professional accountant, while its Ethics Committee tries to make the codes of professional ethics in various countries more compatible with each other. For example, the Education Committee has published *Guidelines* dealing with the education and experience needed to become an accountant, and continuing professional education. The Ethics Committee has developed the *Code of Ethics for Professional Accountants,* which covers, among other items, accountants' integrity, objectivity, and independence, as well as the confidentiality of information obtained during the course of an audit.

Every five years IFAC organizes a World Congress of Accountants, the 15th of which was held in Paris, France, in 1997 and the 16th will be held in Hong Kong in 2002. Eighteen countries are represented on IFAC's governing council, and general assemblies of the organization are conducted every two and a half years. Council terms are also two and a half years.

Acceptance of IFAC pronouncements received a major boost when IOSCO (discussed earlier) voted in 1992 to accept ISAs for purposes of multinational registrations and filings with securities commissions.

IFAC and IASC are closely linked. For example, (1) full membership in IFAC automatically includes membership in IASC; (2) IFAC appoints the 13 country members to IASC's Board; and (3) IFAC contributes to the budget of IASC.

European Union (EU)

The EU, formerly known as the European Community (EC) and at its start as the European Common Market, was formed in 1957 by the Treaty of Rome and now has 15 members: Austria, Belgium, Denmark, Finland, France, Germany, Greece, Ireland, Italy, Luxembourg, the Netherlands, the United Kingdom, Spain, Sweden, and Portugal. The EU's major aims are the free flow of goods, persons, and capital; a customs union; the harmonization of laws; and monetary union. To achieve its objectives, the EU issues various *Directives,* which are EU laws that member states are obligated to incorporate into their own national laws. Since the EU harmonization efforts have the full weight of law behind them, the provisions are mandatory for any company doing business there.

Four EU *Directives* have been issued that have major financial reporting consequences. They are

Fourth Directive, issued July 26, 1978, basically addressing format and content of financial statements (i.e., constituting EU GAAP).

Directive to Publish Interim Financial Statements, issued February 15, 1982, calling for the publication of six months' interim financial reports within four months of the end of an accounting period.

Seventh Directive, issued June 13, 1983, comprehensively addressing the issue of consolidated financial statements.

Eighth Directive, issued April 10, 1984, covering various aspects of the qualifications of professionals authorized to carry out legally required (statutory) audits.

Recall from Chapter 1 there are some fundamental dissimilarities in accounting among the EU countries. For example, the fair presentation/full disclosure model of accounting is found in the United Kingdom, Ireland, and the Netherlands, while the legal compliance model of accounting is found in France, Germany, and Italy. The *Fourth Directive* was a compromise between these two contrasting models of accounting. It contained numerous options that EU member countries could adopt. Still, it succeeded in standardizing the presentation of the income statements and balance sheets and specified minimum disclosures in the footnotes to the financial statements. The *Seventh Directive* was a major advance, since few EU member countries even required consolidated financial statements at the time. (Chapter 6 discusses consolidated statements.) All in all, the *Directives* brought accounting in the EU countries up to a good and fairly comparable level.

The *Eighth Directive* had provisions that would allow auditors from one country to practice in another. Structures were also created to develop what was hoped to be a Europewide market in professional accounting services. Despite good intentions, this development has not really taken place, and Europe remains a segmented market for audit services.

In 1995, the European Commission (which is the governing body of the EU) announced a new accounting harmonization strategy. In a clear break with previous policies, the Commission decided that in the future the EU will support the IASC/IOSCO initiative and work to bring EU accounting requirements in line with IASs *for consolidated financial statements.* The new strategy recognized several realities: (1) The *Fourth* and *Seventh* Directives were incomplete. For example, accounting for foreign currency translation (Chapter 6), pensions, and leases were not covered. (2) The accounting-related *Directives* remained as they were initially issued. As static accounting standards, they were never improved or updated. In other words, change proved to be difficult to implement. (3) With national standards on the one hand and IASs on the other, regional Europewide regulations were seen as an unnecessary third tier. EU *Directives* simply did not help European MNCs who wanted to be listed on several stock exchanges, especially if they wished to list shares in the United States. Despite this new strategy, it is a mistake to say that the EU has lost interest in accounting. Further, should the IASC/IOSCO initiative unravel, the Commission will likely review its decision to refer the harmonization of accounting to IASs.

United Nations

The interest of the United Nations (UN) in accounting and reporting reflects its wider interest in the effects of multinational corporations on the world economy. In 1982, an advisory group reaffirmed a set of *Guidelines* issued in 1977 listing financial and nonfinancial disclosures that multinational corporations ought to provide. Among the suggested financial disclosures are an income statement and balance sheet, expenditures on research and development, and the amounts of new investments in fixed assets. Recommended nonfinancial disclosures include information about employment and transfer pricing policies.

Current financial accounting and reporting endeavors at the UN are carried out by its Intergovernmental Working Group of Experts on International Standards of Accounting and Reporting. The group promulgates "best practices," including those recommended by the IASC, and focuses a great deal of attention on providing technical accounting assistance to developing countries.

Organization for Economic Cooperation and Development

The *Organization for Economic Cooperation and Development* (OECD) is an organization of 29 governments of nearly all industrialized countries: Australia, Austria, Belgium, Canada, Czech Republic, Denmark, Finland, France, Germany, Greece, Hungary, Iceland, Ireland, Italy, Japan, Korea, Luxembourg, Mexico, the Netherlands, New Zealand, Norway, Poland, Portugal, Spain, Sweden, Switzerland, Turkey, the United Kingdom, and the United States. Its purpose is to foster economic growth and development in member countries, and it principally acts as a vehicle whereby member countries consult with each other about general economic matters that concern them all, such as balance of payments or exchange rate problems.

The *OECD Guidelines for Multinational Enterprises* includes recommended voluntary disclosures of financial information. The OECD also looks at the accounting principles in member countries with a view toward encouraging greater harmonization and comparability of accounting and financial reporting. The OECD intends to act only as a catalyst, however. It has neither the resources nor the desire to actually write generally accepted accounting principles. The OECD has periodic conferences and seminars on issues of accounting interest. One of the OECD's primary accounting initiatives of late has been to aid in the accounting and auditing reforms under way in Eastern Europe.

CONCLUSION

As the 21st century begins, the goal of international harmonization of accounting and auditing has been widely accepted. The reason is the globalization of capital markets and the large number of companies listing their shares on "foreign" stock exchanges. Diverse accounting practices used to represent the same reality make little sense as investors everywhere seek comparable financial reporting from companies, no matter where they come from. The debate has moved on from whether harmonization is desirable or practical to how best to achieve it.

The leading contender to establish international accounting standards is the International Accounting Standards Committee. However, events may prove to be the IASC's undoing. One is IOSCO's endorsement of IASs and the core standards. Failure to achieve this endorsement would be a serious blow to the prestige of the IASC. Similarly, the acceptance of IASs by the U.S. SEC is important for maintaining current momentum.[2] The IASC has also proposed a major restructuring. Among other goals, it wants to streamline the way IASs are developed, make the process more open, and formalize the involvement of national accounting standard setters in its operations. However, some critics fear that under the IASC's proposals, continental Europe, and the emerging market nations of Asia, Africa, and South America will lose influence in the standard setting process. They worry that future IASs will only serve the needs of major capital markets and that the IASC will cease to be a truly international body. Nevertheless, the IASC has proved resilient over its history. In your authors' opinion, it will adapt as necessary to maintain its preeminence as the world's accounting standard setter.

REVIEW QUESTIONS

1. What is the difference between accounting standards and auditing standards? How are they interrelated?
2. What is the basic rationale for harmonizing accounting and auditing standards internationally?
3. Chapter 3 describes IASC and IFAC. How are these two international accounting organizations different from one another? In what respects are they similar?
4. Why is IOSCO endorsement of IASC and IFAC pronouncements viewed as important?
5. Why did the EU abandon its approach to accounting harmonization (via Directives) to one favoring the IASC?
6. What roles do the UN and OECD play in harmonizing accounting and auditing standards?
7. What events threaten the IASC's preeminence as the world's accounting standard setter?

CASES

3–1 Let's Go International

Chad Pancoast is at a business luncheon with Mary Jo Dillingham. He is chief financial officer (CFO) of Quaccess.com and she is a Big Five partner in

---

[2]The interested reader should consult the IASC's website (www.iasc.org.uk) for the latest information on these developments.

charge of Quaccess.com's independent audit. They are discussing the makeup of this year's Quaccess.com annual report.

"Our company is becoming more and more internationally oriented," observes Chad. "About 60 percent of our sales are outside the country. We have listed our stock on six different foreign stock exchanges, and we borrow a lot of money from international banks. Maybe the time has come to refer to international accounting standards in our annual report."

Mary Jo cautions by urging careful consideration. She explains, "In the United States, we have no control over IASs. What happens if they come up with a standard simply unacceptable to Quaccess.com? Will you then drop the reference to international standards? That would really be a red flag to financial analysts all over."

"I understand that," Chad counters. "But I like being a trendsetter. Few, if any, U.S. companies refer to IASs and I think we could really draw attention to Quaccess.com if we did that. Why, we'd be in the same league as Nestlé and Bayer—some of the biggest corporate names in the world!"

"I know. I know," says Mary Jo. "It's your annual report for sure. But I really don't see any benefits from referencing IASs—I mainly see risks. Please think carefully before you jump."

Questions

1. Do you support Chad or Mary Jo on this issue? Defend your answer briefly.

2. What are the likely benefits to Quaccess.com from publicly referring to IASC pronouncements?

3. Should the U.S. SEC require all publicly traded U.S. companies to refer to IASs in their respective annual reports? Why or why not?

3–2 Who Uses IASs?

The International Accounting Standards Committee claims that IASC Standards are gaining widespread use and recognition around the world. The IASC website (www.iasc.org.uk) maintains a list of (1) companies that state their financial statements conform to IASs, (2) countries that endorse IASs, and (3) stock exchanges that accept IASs for cross-border listing purposes.

Go the IASC website and find the information on the *acceptability* of International Accounting Standards. Then choose five countries for further analysis. You will use the information on the IASC website to complete this case. Answer the questions below for each of the five countries chosen.

Questions

1. Are IASs endorsed as the national standards? Are IASs allowed to be used in lieu of national standards to prepare financial statements? Must national standards be used (i.e., IASs not allowed) to prepare financial statements?

2. Does the stock exchange allow IASs to be used for purposes of cross-border listing?
3. To which model of accounting does the country belong?
4. What patterns are revealed by your answers to the above questions?

3–3 International Harmonization: Pro or Con?

You are provided the following arguments for and against establishing a harmonized set of international accounting standards:

Pro

Harmonizing accounting standards internationally will improve the comparability of accounting information around the world and thereby eliminate one source of misunderstanding in transnational financial reporting. More comparability will better the analysis of financial statements; this will, in turn, lower interest rates and improve resource allocation. A single set of financial accounting standards will also save corporations time and money, since they will no longer have to prepare multiple sets of financial statements. Finally, establishing international standards will raise the quality of accounting in many countries.

Con

Harmonized international accounting standards internationally are unnecessary, since the worldwide competition for investment funds is propelling harmonization to the extent that investors desire it. Corporations in need of funds are compelled to provide financial statement users—the resource providers—with what they want or else pay a penalty in the form of higher interest rates or lower common stock prices. If user needs are similar internationally, then harmonization will result as a matter of course, without an organized effort. If they are not, then requiring a single set of accounting practices may actually worsen the situation. Accounting is relevant only when it is responsive to the environment in which it operates. Imposing harmonization could very well strip accounting of its usefulness in many situations.

Question

Write two paragraphs stating your position on the desirability of establishing a harmonized set of international accounting standards.

ADDITIONAL READINGS

Carey, A. H. "Toward a Common Language." *Financial Executive,* November/December 1996, pp. 38–41.

de Reyna, R. "UNCTAD's Activities in Accountancy Development." *IFAC Newsletter* (June 1995), pp. 5–6. (Note: UNCTAD is the United Nations Conference on Trade and Development.)

Hegarty, J. "Accounting for the Global Economy: Is National Regulation Doomed to Disappear?" *Accounting Horizons,* December 1997, pp. 75–90.

Hora, J. A., R. H. Tondkar, and A. Adhikari. "International Accounting Standards in Capital Markets." *Journal of International Accounting Auditing & Taxation* 6, no. 2 (1997), pp. 171–90.

McGregor, W. "An Insider's View of the Current State and Future of International Accounting Standard Setting." *Accounting Horizons,* June 1999, pp. 159–68.

Morris, D. C., and G. M. Ward. *One Global Corporate Reporting Standard: Nightmare? Dream? Or Reality?* New York: PricewaterhouseCoopers, May 1999. 14 pp.

Saudagaran, S. M., and J. G. Diga. "Accounting Harmonization in ASEAN: Benefits, Models and Policy Issues." *Journal of International Accounting Auditing & Taxation* 7, no. 1 (1998), pp. 21–45.

Street, D. L., and K. A. Shaughnessy. "The Evolution of the G4+1 and Its Impact on International Harmonization of Accounting Standards." *Journal of International Accounting Auditing & Taxation* 7, no. 2 (1998), pp. 131–61.

Walton, P. "European Harmonization." In *International Accounting and Finance Handbook,* 2nd ed., 1999 Supplement, ed. F. D. S. Choi. New York: John Wiley & Sons, 1999, pp. 11.1–11.14.

Zeff, S. A. "The Coming Confrontation on International Accounting Standards." *The Irish Accounting Review,* Autumn 1998, pp. 89–117.

4

FINANCIAL REPORTING IN THE INTERNATIONAL ENVIRONMENT

LEARNING OBJECTIVES

1. Define transnational financial reporting and explain what has caused the phenomenon.
2. Understand the difficulties involved when accounting information is transmitted internationally.
3. Identify actions that investors can take when they receive financial reports prepared using an unfamiliar language, monetary unit, or set of accounting standards.
4. Distinguish five approaches that multinational corporations take to accommodate foreign readers of their financial reports and evaluate the advantages and disadvantages of each approach.
5. Appreciate why financial statement users must be careful when comparing accounting information of companies from different countries.

Financial accounting practices in a country are determined by a number of environmental variables that interact in a complex way. As discussed in Chapter 1, these variables include the following:

1. External finance.
2. Legal system.

3. Political and economic ties with other countries.

4. Level of inflation.

5. Size and complexity of business enterprises, sophistication of management and the financial community, and general levels of education.

6. Culture.

Companies prepare the financial statements in their annual report directed toward the needs of their primary users. Financial statements not only look different but report different information, depending on whether the primary user group is, for example, the shareholder, the creditor, or the government. Moreover, even if companies in different nations orient their financial statements toward similar user groups, there are still likely to be differences in accounting practices and in the way that the annual reports appear. For example, companies from the United States and Great Britain orient their annual reports to the decision needs of shareholders, but there are still a number of differences in the two countries' accounting and reporting practices.

Transnational financial reporting refers to reporting across national boundaries or, more specifically, to reporting financial results to user groups located in a country other than the one where the company is headquartered. A U.S. company is engaged in transnational financial reporting whenever it sends an annual report to a citizen of another country. If you write to a German company and receive its annual report, transnational financial reporting has occurred.

Transnational financial reporting has been encouraged by two phenomena. The first may be termed the *global financing strategies* of multinational corporations. Global financing includes (1) listing a company's capital stock on stock exchanges outside the home country, (2) selling bonds in various countries, and (3) arranging for loans with foreign banks. Multinational corporations no longer look exclusively to the stock markets, bond markets, and banks of their respective home countries to raise capital. They go wherever the money is most available and cheapest. The second phenomenon is *transnational investing;* those with funds to invest buy the stocks and bonds of foreign companies in addition to those in their own nation. Thus, the multinational corporation (as the resource user) and the shareholder/creditor (as the resource provider) are responsible for these twin phenomena.

A truly global financial market began to emerge in the 1980s, and it has continued to grow ever since. Exhibit 4–1 shows that the increase in international financial transactions is rather startling because it has more than doubled between 1993 and 1997.

Transnational financial reporting presents a unique problem to both the multinational corporation (as the information provider) and the shareholder/creditor (as the information user). When a company prepares a financial report for users in its own country, it can reasonably assume that the users understand (1) the general orientation of financial accounting in that country, (2) the particular

---

EXHIBIT 4–1   International Financing Activity on World Capital Markets by Type of Instrument (amounts in $billions)

	1993	1994	1995	1996	1997
Bonds	481.0	428.6	467.3	708.8	831.6
Equities	40.7	45.0	41.0	57.7	85.1
Syndicated loans[a]	136.7	236.2	370.2	345.2	390.4
Other debt facilities	8.2	4.9	3.8	4.5	2.7
Total	**666.6**	**714.7**	**882.3**	**1,116.2**	**1,309.8**

[a] A *syndicated bank loan* is one in which a group of banks provides funds to the borrower. A group of banks is needed because the borrower may seek an amount too large (in terms of credit risk) for a single bank to manage.

SOURCE: Organization for Economic Cooperation and Development (OECD), *Financial Market Trends* 69 (February 1998), Paris, 1998.

accounting practices that the company employs, (3) the language in which the annual report is written, and (4) the currency unit used to present the financial statements. However, any or all of these four items may be different when a company sends a financial report to users in another country. More and more corporations and investors are facing transnational financial reporting problems as both financing and investing are increasingly globalized.

RESPONSES BY USERS

Exhibit 4–2 is the 1998 income statement for the German retailer, Karstadt. Suppose that a friend of yours suggests that Karstadt would be a good company to invest in, and so you write Karstadt, and ask for and receive its annual report. What would immediately strike you after opening the annual report is that it is written entirely in German. In looking at the financial statements, you also notice that all of the amounts are expressed in deutsche marks (DM). The report looks different from U.S. companies' reports (compare Exhibit 4–2 to Exhibit 4–3, the 1998 income statement of Safeway, Inc.), so you may also suspect that Karstadt uses German accounting practices. Unless you can read German, know German accounting practices, and are familiar with the mark, you will probably have a difficult time understanding Karstadt's annual report. As a result, you may decide not to invest in Karstadt since it would be "too much trouble" to extract the information you need from the annual report. You may very well pass up a good investment opportunity, although you will never know it.

Of course, you may also take other courses of action. One would be to get someone to translate the report into English, while you learn all you can about German accounting practices. (Several large CPA firms publish such information, and books are also available on the subject.) At a minimum, this choice would be time-consuming and could even cost you money if you had to pay someone for the

EXHIBIT 4–2   Karstadt Income Statement

Gewinn- und Verlustrechnung

	ergebnisbezogene Veränderungen in TDM	ergebnisbezogene Veränderungen in %
1. Umsatzerlöse		
Umsätze netto	−5.154.428	− 21,67
2. Sonstige betriebliche Erträge	17.996	1,79
3. Materialaufwand	4.095.200	28,11
4. Personalaufwand	232.487	4,79
5. Abschreibungen auf immaterielle Vermögensgegenstände des Anlagevermögens und Sachanlagen	24.210	3,56
6. Sonstige betriebliche Aufwendungen	719.938	16,40
7. Beteiligungsergebnis	60.417	231,23
8. Abschreibungen auf Finanzanlagen	2.071	99,57
9. Zinsergebnis	− 26.184	− 60,61
10. Ergebnis der gewöhnlichen Geschäftstätigkeit	**− 28.293**	**− 10,21**
11. Steuern vom Einkommen und vom Ertrag	27.189	47,65
12. Sonstige Steuern	1.080	1,93
13. Jahresüberschuß	**− 24**	**− 0,01**

Der Konsolidierung sind testierte Jahresabschlüsse zugrunde gelegt. Der *C-&-N-Touristic-Konzern* wurde mit dem Rumpfgeschäftsjahr 01.01. bis 31.10.1998 nach der Equity-Methode erfaßt.

translation. And having done this, the accounting information would still not be directly comparable to that of a U.S. company. In most cases, it is impossible for a *user* to restate financial accounting information so that it conforms to the accounting practices of another country. Another course of action is to forgo trying to understand the Karstadt annual report and instead rely on the advice of an expert, such as a stockbroker. In fact, investment firms employ people to analyze foreign companies' annual reports and to make recommendations about which companies seem to be good ones to invest in. Such analysis involves a high level of sophistication.

Many accountants are concerned about the effects that an unfamiliar language, monetary unit, and accounting practices may have on investors and creditors. They fear that resource allocation decisions may be based on misunderstanding and, as a result, that these decisions may not be optimal. This is one reason why accountants are trying to harmonize accounting practices around the world. (This effort is discussed in Chapter 3.)

EXHIBIT 4–3   Safeway Inc. Income Statement

CONSOLIDATED STATEMENTS OF INCOME (In millions, except per-share amounts)	52 Weeks 1998	53 Weeks 1997	52 Weeks 1996
Sales	$24,484.2	$22,483.8	$17,269.0
Cost of goods sold	(17,359.7)	(16,069.1)	(12,494.8)
Gross Profit	7,124.5	6,414.7	4.774.2
Operating and administrative expense	(5,522.8)	(5,135.0)	(3,882.5)
Operating Profit	1,601.7	1,279.7	891.7
Interest expense	(235.0)	(241.2)	(178.5)
Equity in earnings of unconsolidated affiliates	28.5	34.9	50.0
Other income, net	1.7	2.9	4.4
Income before Income Taxes and Extraordinary Loss	1,396.9	1,076.3	767.6
Income taxes	(590.2)	(454.8)	(307.0)
Income before Extraordinary Loss	806.7	621.5	460.6
Extraordinary loss related to early retirement of debt, net of income tax benefit of $41.1	—	(64.1)	—
Net Income	$ 806.7	$ 557.4	$ 460.6
Basic Earnings per Share:			
Income before extraordinary loss	$ 1.67	$ 1.35	$ 1.06
Extraordinary loss	—	(0.14)	—
Net Income	$ 1.67	$ 1.21	$ 1.06
Diluted Earnings per Share:			
Income before extraordinary loss	$ 1.59	$ 1.25	$ 0.97
Extraordinary loss	—	(0.13)	—
Net Income	$ 1.59	$ 1.12	$ 0.97
Weighted Average Shares Outstanding—Basic	482.8	462.3	436.0
Weighted Average Shares Outstanding—Diluted	508.8	497.7	475.7

See accompanying notes to consolidated financial statements.

RESPONSES BY MULTINATIONAL CORPORATIONS

What about multinational corporations? Don't they have a role to play in trying to minimize misunderstandings? Indeed they do. Just as the users of financial reports may take various courses of action to overcome the problems associated with transnational financial reporting, so too do companies approach the problems in various ways. We can classify five approaches that multinational corporations take to accommodate foreign readers of their financial reports:

1. Do nothing.
2. Prepare convenience translations.
3. Prepare convenience statements.
4. Restate on a limited basis.
5. Prepare secondary financial statements.

EXHIBIT 4–4   Multinational Corporations' Approaches to Transnational Financial
Reporting

	Language	*Currency*	*GAAP*
Do nothing	H	H	H
Convenience translation	O	H	H
Convenience statement	O	H & O	H
Limited restatement	O	H[1]	H & O
Secondary financial statements	O	H[1]	H/O[2]

Key: H = Home country (i.e., domestic)
   O = Other

[1]Normally H; sometimes H & O.

[2] Primary financial statements based on home GAAP; secondary financial statements most often based on IAS or U.S. GAAP.

Exhibit 4–4 provides a summary of the change in language, currency, or GAAP that each different approach requires.

Do Nothing

A corporation that sends the same financial statements to the foreign user as it does to the domestic user has done nothing to accommodate the foreign user. The financial statements are written in the native language and use the native currency unit and accounting principles. This approach puts the entire burden of understanding the financial report on the user, and it more or less assumes that the report for readers at home is useful to readers in other countries as well. The income statements for both Karstadt and Safeway illustrate the do-nothing approach.

Why would a corporation choose to seemingly ignore the information needs of its foreign readers? First of all, if the company raises very little capital outside the borders of its home country, the added expense of taking one of the other four approaches may not be worthwhile. While global financing is becoming more commonplace, many corporations that manufacture and sell products multinationally still raise most of their capital in a single nation—the home country. These companies perceive little benefit in preparing financial statements for readers other than those at home.

Second, some multinationals are able to entice international investment in their securities even though they leave their financial statements in their original form. One way they accomplish this is by selling large blocks of their securities directly to sophisticated overseas investors, such as pension funds. (Such sales are called *private placements.*) Or they may meet directly with investment firms, referred to earlier, to encourage the firms to recommend investments in their securities. Large investment firms, especially, employ analysts who are skilled at interpreting financial statements in their original form. Either way, these multinationals attempt to attract foreign investors without incurring the extra costs associated with the other forms of transnational financial reporting.

A third reason why a multinational corporation may choose to do nothing is that the language, currency unit, and accounting principles of its home country are well known and understood around the world. This is true, for example, of U.S. and U.K. companies, which almost always take this approach. U.S. and U.K. accounting standards are highly regarded and generally understood in other parts of the world. Both the U.S. dollar and the British pound are international currencies, and the English language is referred to as the "language of business." Thus, financial reports useful to native readers may very well be useful to foreign readers.

Microsoft is an exception to the norm for a U.S. company. On Microsoft's website *(http://microsoft.com/msft/tools.htm),* you can view Microsoft income statements presented in local languages, currencies, and accounting conventions for Australia, Canada, France, the Netherlands, and the United Kingdom.

Prepare Convenience Translations

Convenience translations are financial statements translated into the foreign reader's language. They retain the home country's accounting principles and currency unit, however. Exhibit 4–5 (p. 59) is an example of this approach. It is the income statement of American Israeli Paper Mills Ltd., Israel's leading producer of paper. Note that while the income statement is in English, it still uses Israeli accounting principles and the Israeli shekel.

This approach is a relatively inexpensive accommodation to the foreign readership. Companies taking this approach typically prepare English, French, German, and, perhaps, Spanish language versions (as appropriate) of their annual reports. Presumably, any interested reader will understand one of these languages. The user is saved the bother of dealing with an unfamiliar language but must still understand another country's accounting practices and monetary unit. Companies usually prepare convenience translations in order to enlarge the scope of shareholder/creditor interest beyond the borders of their home country, and they are a low-cost alternative to the do-nothing approach. For this reason, convenience translations are also commonly used with private placements or to attract the attention of foreign investment firms, as discussed previously.

Prepare Convenience Statements

This approach takes convenience translations one step further. Not only are the financial statements translated into the language of the foreign reader, but the monetary amounts are also expressed in the reader's currency. However, the accounting principles of the home country are still used to prepare the financial reports. Exhibit 4–6 is an example of a convenience statement for Suzuki Motor Corporation, a Japanese designer and manufacturer of motorized vehicles. (Notice that yen amounts are translated into dollars at the fiscal year-end exchange rate.

EXHIBIT 4–5   American Israeli Paper Mills Ltd.

CONSOLIDATED STATEMENTS OF INCOME
In Adjusted New Israeli Shekels

In Thousands	Note	**1998**	*1997*	*1996*
Net Sales	10g	**1,451,819**	1,442,313	1,408,717
Cost of Sales	10h	**1,153,463**	1,151,900	1,155,751
Gross Profit		**298,356**	290,413	252,966
Selling and Marketing, Administrative and General Expenses:	10i			
Selling and marketing		**132,925**	132,367	118,073
Administrative and general		**63,872**	65,932	59,535
		196,797	198,299	177,608
Income from Ordinary Operations		**101,559**	92,114	75,358
Financial Expenses (Income)—net	10j	**491**	(8,541)	8,424
Income Before Taxes on Income		**101,068**	100,655	66,934
Taxes on Income	7	**31,911**	27,718	10,401
Income from Operations of the Company and its Subsidiaries		**69,157**	72,937	56,533
Other Income—Capital Gain on Decrease in Holding in Subsidiary due to Issuance of Shares to a Third Party		**16,640**		52,716
Share in Profits (Losses) of Associated Companies—net	2	**1,868**	(831)	6,681
Minority Interest in Profits of Subsidiaries		**(24,982)**	(22,381)	(11,310)
Net Income for the Year		**62,683**	49,725	104,620
			Adjusted NIS	
Net Income per NIS 1 of Par Value of Shares	1n;11	**1,626**	1,302	2,749

The accompanying notes are an integral part of the financial statements.

An exchange rate is simply how much of one currency it takes to buy so much of another currency. At Suzuki's year-end, the exchange rate was Yen 132.10 = U.S. $1.00, and so all amounts initially expressed in yen are simply divided by 132.10 to arrive at the dollar figures.)

Convenience statements often lose much of their foreign appearance, and unless users realize that another country's accounting principles are used, they will

---

EXHIBIT 4–6   Suzuki Motor Corporation Income Statement

CONSOLIDATED STATEMENTS OF INCOME
Years Ended 31st March, 1998 and 1997

Suzuki Motor Corporation and Consolidated Subsidiaries	*Millions of Yen*		*Thousands of U.S. Dollars*
	1998	*1997*	*1998*
Net Sales	**¥1,488,785**	¥1,502,424	**$11,270,139**
Cost of Sales	**1,133,128**	1,154,184	**8,577,807**
Gross profit	**355,657**	348,240	**2,692,332**
Selling, General and Administrative Expenses	**299,048**	280,138	**2,263,803**
Operating income	**56,608**	68,101	**428,529**
Other Income (expenses):			
Interest and dividend income	**4,339**	4,106	**32,848**
Interest expense	**(6,195)**	(7,884)	**(46,897)**
Other, net	**(1,201)**	4,472	**(9,098)**
Income before income taxes	**53,550**	68,796	**405,382**
Income Taxes:			
Current (Note 9)	**38,812**	46,082	**293,810**
Deferred	**(4,303)**	(1,329)	**(32,577)**
	34,508	44,752	**261,233**
Equity Items:			
Minority interests in earnings of consolidated subsidiaries	**(830)**	(837)	**(6,287)**
Equity in earnings of non-consolidated subsidiaries and affiliates	**12,654**	11,047	**95,796**
Other (Adjustments on consolidated subsidiaries)	**(709)**	(667)	**(5,370)**
Net income	**¥ 30,156**	¥ 33,586	**$ 228,287**

	Yen		*U.S. dollars*
Net Income per Share:			
Primary	**¥67.17**	¥74.84	**$0.508**
Fully diluted	**66.71**	74.29	**0.504**
Cash Dividends per Share	**7.50**	8.50	**0.056**

The accompanying Notes to Consolidated Financial Statements are an integral part of these statements.

be misled into thinking that the financial statements can be directly compared to those of companies of their home country. Naturally, readers can comprehend their own language and currency better than those of another country, but they must still be able to understand the accounting practices used in the *company's home country* in order to derive actual meaning from the annual report.

Restate on a Limited Basis

Compared to the first three, this approach represents a significant step toward accommodating the information needs of foreign readers. The disclosure is in the footnotes section of the company's financial statements. Normally, a company reconciles the net income amount shown on its income statement (prepared using its home-country accounting principles) to a net income amount based on the accounting principles of the reader's country, and often the company restates the balance sheet figures as well. However, sometimes a company restates only selected financial statement items. The annual report is typically written in the reader's language, but the currency is still that of the company's country.

Companies adopting this approach feel a clear need to communicate with their foreign annual report users. If a significant number of shareholders or creditors is located in other countries and if the company's accounting practices diverge significantly from those found in the reader's country, then the need is real. Companies following this approach must keep more than one set of accounting records. Fortunately computerized accounting systems can significantly reduce the cost and inconvenience of this approach!

A number of companies adopt this approach. The disclosure of the Finnish company Valmet in Exhibit 4–7 (p. 62) is illustrative. Notice that Valmet reconciles both net income and shareholders' equity from Finnish to U.S. accounting principles.

Prepare Secondary Financial Statements

This represents a further accommodation to the users of a company's financial statements. Companies continue to prepare their primary financial statements for the home user with the home country's language, currency, and accounting principles. For foreign readers, however, the company completely restates its financial report to conform to another set of accounting standards.

In practice, the other set of accounting standards used most often is either the generally accepted accounting principles (GAAP) of the United States or the standards of the International Accounting Standards Committee (IASC). U.S. GAAP are the most detailed and extensive in the world, and they are generally regarded as "world class" in quality. As a result, many multinationals choose U.S. GAAP when they prepare their secondary financial statements. However, as discussed in Chapter 3, the IASC is increasingly accepted as the voice for acceptable worldwide accounting standards. (As a practical matter, there are few significant instances where U.S. GAAP conflict with IASC Standards.) Japanese multinationals preparing secondary financial statements tend to use U.S. GAAP,

---

EXHIBIT 4–7   Valmet Limited Restatement (from Finnish to U.S. accounting
principles; amounts in millions of Finnish Markkas)

---

(26) U.S. GAAP Information

The accompanying consolidated financial statements have been prepared in accordance with Finnish GAAP, which differs in certain significant respects from U.S. GAAP. The following is a summary of the adjustments to net income and shareholders' equity that would have been required if U.S. GAAP had been applied instead of Finnish GAAP in the preparation of the consolidated financial statements.

	Group	
(FIM millions, except per share amounts)	*1997*	*1998*
Net income under Finnish GAAP	863	675
Adjustments to reconcile to U.S. GAAP:		
Pensions (a)	5	−75
Income taxes (b)	−28	18
Goodwill (c)	10	11
Investments (e)	25	9
Capitalization of interest (f)	−1	4
Equity method investees (g)	−9	—
Tax effect of U.S. GAAP adjustments	−8	17
Net income under U.S. GAAP	857	659
Basic earnings per share (h)	10.97	8.44

	Group	
	Dec. 31, 1997	*Dec. 31, 1998*
Shareholders' equity under Finnish GAAP	3 893	4 222
Pensions (a)	−190	−294
Income taxes (b)	71	106
Goodwill (c)	−82	−71
Revaluations (d)	−70	−70
Investments (e)	102	32
Capitalization of interest (f)	42	46
Shareholders' equity under U.S. GAAP	3 766	3 971

---

whereas European multinationals that prepare secondary financial statements tend to adopt IASC Standards.

Secondary financial statements are meant for sophisticated worldwide users. What makes a company go to so much trouble to accommodate the foreign reader? As with the previous approaches, it all comes down to whether the perceived benefits exceed the costs. Multinationals preparing secondary financial statements are normally from countries where accounting is legalistic in its orientation. For them, the fair presentation/full disclosure model of accounting, with its emphasis on presenting useful information to shareholders and creditors, is more likely to attract widespread international investment than is their home country's legal compliance model of accounting. (IASC Standards and, of course, U.S. GAAP reflect the fair presentation/full disclosure model of accounting discussed in Chapter 1.)

Exhibit 4–8 (p. 64) is the 1998 consolidated income statement of Canon Inc., the Japanese camera manufacturer. Notice that three years' worth of data are presented in Japanese yen, while the 1998 amounts are translated into U.S. dollars using the year-end exchange rate. Exhibit 4–8 also reproduces Canon's footnote indicating that U.S. GAAP are used. Exhibit 4–9 (p. 65) is the 1998 consolidated income statement of the Swiss pharmaceutical company Roche. Two years' worth of data are presented in Swiss francs. The footnote describing the use of IASC Standards is also reproduced in Exhibit 4–9.

WHOSE ACCOUNTING PRINCIPLES?

Restating financial statements to another set of accounting standards, as in limited restatements and secondary financial statements, has its critics. Some believe that financial statements are meaningful only if they are consistent with the underlying environmental variables from which accounting in a company's home country is derived. (The variables affecting accounting development are discussed in Chapter 1.) According to this view, the first three forms of transnational financial reporting make more sense, since they retain the accounting principles of the company's home country. In essence, the argument is that the effects of business decisions, as reflected in financial statements, cannot be separated from the accounting principles used to measure and originally record these decisions. The alternative view is that comparability improves shareholder decision making, and so one of the last two forms of transnational financial reporting is more appropriate. This conceptual conflict presents a dilemma for both users and multinational corporations involved in international financial reporting.

BEWARE THE FOREIGN FINANCIAL STATEMENT

So far, we have discussed the problems confronted by financial statement users when they are provided information that is not in their native language, their native currency, or prepared according to accustomed accounting principles. We have also discussed what corporations do to help financial statement users overcome these problems. Even if readers get financial statements in a language, currency unit, and based on accounting principles that they can understand, they must still consider that the inherent reliability of financial statements can vary because of different auditing standards worldwide. (This issue was discussed in Chapter 3.)

EXHIBIT 4–8   Canon Income Statement

Canon Inc. and Subsidiaries

CONSOLIDATED STATEMENTS OF INCOME

Years ended December 31, 1998, 1997 and 1996

	Millions of Yen			Thousands of U.S. Dollars (note 2)
	1998	*1997*	*1996*	*1998*
Net sales	¥2,826,269	2,761,025	2,558,227	$24,364,388
Cost of sales	1,569,197	1,528,364	1,465,437	13,527,560
Gross profit	1,257,072	1,232,661	1,092,790	10,836,828
Selling, general and administrative expenses	996,294	958,627	871,754	8,588,742
Operating profit	260,778	274,034	221,036	2,248,086
Other income (deductions):				
Interest and dividend income	12,576	13,922	12,972	108,414
Interest expense	(28,881)	(29,789)	(33,844)	(248,974)
Other, net	(4,960)	(23,362)	(17,399)	(42,759)
	(21,265)	(39,229)	(38,271)	(183,319)
Income before income taxes and minority interests	239,513	234,805	182,765	2,064,767
Income taxes (note 11)	123,843	109,364	80,636	1,067,612
Income before minority interests	115,670	125,441	102,129	997,155
Minority interests	6,101	6,628	7,952	52,595
Net income	¥ 109,569	118,813	94,177	$ 944,560
	Yen			U.S. dollars (note 2)
Net income per share (notes 1[p] and 16):				
Basic	¥ 126.10	137.73	111.29	$ 1.09
Diluted	123.93	134.60	106.96	1.07
Dividends per common share (note 13)	¥ 17.00	17.00	15.00	$ 0.15

See accompanying notes to consolidated financial statements.

Note: Basis of Presentation
The Company and its domestic subsidiaries maintain their books of account in conformity with financial accounting standards of Japan. Foreign subsidiaries maintain their books in conformity with financial accounting standards of the countries of their domicile.

The accompanying consolidated financial statements reflect the adjustments which management believes are necessary to conform them with United States generally accepted accounting principles except for Statement of Financial Accounting Standards No. 115, "Accounting for Certain Investments in Debt and Equity Securities" (see note 4).

EXHIBIT 4–9   Roche Income Statement

CONSOLIDATED STATEMENTS OF INCOME
For years ended 31 December

In millions of CHF (Swiss francs)

	1998	*1997*
Sales[3]	**24,662**	18,767
Cost of sales	**(7,901)**	(6,091)
Gross profit	**16,761**	12,676
Marketing and distribution	**(6,774)**	(5,060)
Research and development[3]	**(3,408)**	(2,903)
Administration	**(1,053)**	(876)
Other operating income (expense), net[5]	**(1,176)**	(247)
Operating profit	**4,350**	3,590
Non-operating income (expense), net[6]	**1,083**	1,577
Result before special charges and taxes	**5,433**	5,167
Special charges[2]		
Acquired in-process research and development	—	(4,445)
Restructuring	—	(2,981)
Result before taxes	**5,433**	(2,259)
Income taxes[7]		
On result before special charges	**(965)**	(830)
Benefit from special charges	—	1,118
Income applicable to minority interests[20]	**(76)**	(60)
Net income (loss)	**4,392**	(2,031)

Note: Basis of preparation of financial statements
The consolidated financial statements of the Roche Group are prepared in accordance with
International Accounting Standards under the historical cost convention. Standards that are effective
for the year ended 31 December 1998 have been taken into consideration.

Finally, it should be noted that financial practices (as opposed to accounting practices) and business decision making differ around the world, and readers of foreign financial statements must understand how the business environment in a corporation's home country affects the firm's financial reports. This is especially critical if the user is comparing the accounting numbers of companies from different cultures.

One device used to analyze financial reports is *ratio analysis*. Ratios of key items on the financial statements are calculated to determine such things as riskiness, ability to pay off debts, and profitability. For example, a commonly employed ratio is the debt/asset ratio (total liabilities divided by total assets). Since liabilities must be paid off with company assets, the lower this ratio is, the greater is the company's ability to pay off its debts and, therefore, the safer the company is perceived to be. Generally speaking, creditors should be more willing to lend money to, and shareholders should be more willing to invest money in, companies with lower debt/asset ratios.

However, applying ratio analysis internationally can be deceptive. For example, Japanese companies tend to have significantly higher debt/asset ratios than comparable U.S. companies, even after Japanese financial statements are restated to conform to U.S. accounting principles. In Japan, the debt/asset ratio is an indication of how much confidence the banks have in a company. Companies have low debt/asset ratios because they are unable to get any more credit from the banks. Rather than demonstrating a risky company, in Japan the reverse is true—companies with high debt/asset ratios are generally safer![1]

What this tells us is that comparability still may not exist even if financial statements are prepared on the basis of comparable accounting standards. Because many business practices are culturally based, they are bound to have an impact on companies' financial statements. One must know something about the business environment of a company's home country in order to fully understand the company's financial statements.

International financial statement analysis is explained more fully in Chapter 7.

CONCLUSION

Transnational financial reporting arises when a corporation sends its financial statements to users residing and working in other countries. When this happens, one issue that the corporation faces is that the financial statements it prepares for users in its own country may not serve the needs of users in another part of the world. Financial statements are a communications device, and when a company does not communicate effectively with its audience, it pays a penalty. The penalty arises because failure to fully understand a multinational corporation's financial statements (in whole or in part) increases the risk associated with providing capital to that multinational. When the communications breakdown is severe, the resource providers simply refuse to provide funds to the multinational. However, less extreme penalties that the corporation may pay are higher interest costs or lower common stock prices. The multinational will accommodate its foreign audience if it believes that it can reduce the penalties of nonaccommodation. How the company responds to information needs depends on how it views its own cost/benefit equation—the company will try to balance the increased cost of

---

[1]Frederick D. S. Choi et al., "Analyzing Foreign Financial Statements: The Use and Misuse of International Ratio Analysis," *Journal of International Business Studies,* Spring/Summer 1983, pp. 113–31. Reprinted with permission.

additional accommodation to its financial statement users against the potentially lower penalties that the users may impose.

REVIEW QUESTIONS

1. What is transnational financial reporting and why has it become an issue for many multinational corporations?

2. Why does transnational financial reporting present problems to both users and providers of financial accounting information?

3. What can users do to overcome the problems identified in question 2?

4. What happens when a multinational corporation fails to effectively communicate financial information to its foreign readers?

5. Describe the five approaches that multinational corporations take to accommodate their foreign readers. What are the advantages and disadvantages of each approach?

6. Which approaches to transnational financial reporting retain the accounting standards of the company's home country and which approaches restate financial statement information to another set of accounting principles? What is the main argument for retaining home country accounting standards in transnational financial reporting? What is the main argument favoring restatement?

7. Why must a financial statement user be careful when comparing financial ratios of companies from different countries?

CASES

4–1 What If Suzuki Lists on the NYSE?

Suppose the Suzuki Board of Directors decided that it wanted to list Suzuki stock on the New York Stock Exchange (NYSE).

| NYSE website | *http://www.nyse.com/* |
| Suzuki website | *http://www.suzuki.co.jp/* |

Questions

1. Which example of transnational financial reporting is Suzuki practicing now? Use the Suzuki website to find out why this is so.

2. Why might Suzuki's board of directors want to list Suzuki stock on the NYSE? Use the NYSE website to help you answer this question.

3. What changes to Suzuki's financial statements would have to be made in order for Suzuki's stock to be listed on the NYSE?

4–2 The Mexican Investment

"Holy cow," thought Roger. "What do I do now?"

For some time Roger Chope had been considering investing in a few shares of a foreign company. Because he had heard so much about the positive effects of the North American Free Trade Agreement, he though he would get in on the ground floor by buying some shares of Mexican companies likely to benefit from the agreement.

Roger mailed letters to a number of Mexican firms, asking for a copy of their most recent annual reports. He figured that after analyzing the financial statements he would be able to choose the best one.

He anxiously awaited the responses, but the first one he received was nothing like what he expected. "It's all in Spanish," he thought with dismay. (Roger's knowledge of Spanish ended with ordering beer and locating the public facilities.) "I can't even tell the balance sheet from the income statement. Let's see—pesos . . . Oh yeah, that's the Mexican currency, but I can't remember how many pesos it takes to get a dollar. Analyzing this company is going to be tougher than I realized."

Questions

1. Which example of transnational financial reporting is Roger confronting here? Why might this Mexican company take this approach?
2. What must Roger do to make the financial statements more understandable?
3. Where can he go to learn about Mexican accounting principles?

4–3 Investor's Choice

In this chapter, we have looked at five approaches that MNCs take to accommodate foreign readers of their financial reports. Now, suppose you are a prospective investor and you are interested in the seven companies listed below:

Approach	*Country*	*Company*	*Website*
Do nothing	Germany	Karstadt	*www.karstadt.de*
Convenience translation	Israel	American Israeli Paper Mills	*www.aipm.co.il*
Convenience statement	Japan	Suzuki Motor Corp	*www.suzuki.co.jp*
Limited restatement	Finland	Valmet	*www.valmet.com*
Secondary financial statements	Japan	Canon	*www.canon.com*
	Switzerland	Roche	*www.roche.com*
	United States of America	Microsoft	*www.microsoft.com*

Questions

1. List five items of information you would like to have from each company in order to decide whether or not you will invest in the company's stock.

2. Where will you get the information you have listed for question 1?

3. How much of the information were you able to find for each company?

ADDITIONAL READINGS

Dumontier, P., and B. Raffournier. "Why Firms Comply Voluntarily with IAS: An Empirical Analysis with Swiss Data." *Journal of International Financial Management & Accounting* 9, no. 4 (1998), pp. 216–45.

Frost, C. A., and K. P. Ramin. "Corporate Financial Disclosure: A Global Assessment." In *International Accounting and Finance Handbook*, ed. F. D. S. Choi, 2nd ed. New York: John Wiley & Sons, 1997, pp. 18:1–33.

Frost, C. A., and G. Pownall. "Interdependencies in the Global Markets for Capital and Information: The Case of SmithKline Beecham plc." *Accounting Horizons,* March 1996, pp. 38–57.

Gornik-Tomaszewski, S., and H. H. Meier. "Reporting Practices of Foreign Firms Listed in the United States." *Research in Accounting Regulation,* Supplement 1 (1997), pp. 75–95.

Gray, S. J.; G. K. Meek; and C. B. Roberts. "International Capital Market Pressures and Voluntary Annual Report Disclosures by U.S. and U.K. Multinationals." *Journal of International Financial Management & Accounting,* Spring 1995, pp. 43–68.

Radebaugh, L. H.; G. Gebhardt; and S. J. Gray. "Foreign Stock Exchange Listings: A Case Study of Daimler-Benz." *Journal of International Financial Management & Accounting* 6, no. 2 (1995), pp. 158–92.

Saudagaran, S., and J. G. Diga. "Financial Reporting in Emerging Capital Markets: Characteristics and Policy Issues." *Accounting Horizons* 1, no. 2 (1997), pp. 41–64.

Saudagaran, S. M., and G. K. Meek. "A Review of Research on the Relationship between International Capital Markets and Financial Reporting by Multinational Firms." *Journal of Accounting Literature* 16 (1997), pp. 127–59.

Wallace, R., and K. Naser. "Firm-specific Determinants of the Comprehensiveness of Mandatory Disclosure in the Corporate Annual Reports of Firms Listed on the Stock Exchange of Hong Kong." *Journal of Accounting and Public Policy* 14 (1995), pp. 311–68.

Zarzeski, M. T. "Spontaneous Harmonization Effects of Culture and Market Forces on Accounting Disclosure Practices." *Accounting Horizons,* March 1996, pp. 18–37.

5

DISCLOSURE PRACTICES AROUND THE WORLD

LEARNING OBJECTIVES

1. Distinguish financial and nonfinancial disclosures.
2. Understand the incentives for voluntarily disclosing additional information beyond that required by generally accepted accounting principles.
3. Compare segment disclosures of U.S. and non-U.S. multinational corporations.
4. Introduce certain disclosure innovations from Europe.
5. Assess the trends in disclosure practices in multinational corporations and examine the reasons for them.

The term *disclosure,* in its broadest sense, encompasses the release of any piece of information about a particular company. It includes everything contained in the company's annual report, press releases, newspaper and magazine stories, and so on. However, this chapter is more narrowly focused. It is about disclosures contained in annual reports or, more specifically, annual report information besides that in the main financial statements—the balance sheet, income statement, and statement of cash flows. (While the latter is becoming increasingly common worldwide, it is still not required in all countries.)

Measurement issues are concerned with how financial statements should be prepared, which generally accepted accounting principles (GAAP) to employ, and how assets and liabilities are to be valued. Several substantive international accounting measurement issues are discussed in Chapter 2. *Disclosure* issues, on the other hand, relate to the information in an annual report that supplements the financial statements.

If you obtain the annual report of a U.S. company, you typically find a number of supplemental disclosures:

1. A letter from the company president or chairman of the board explaining the major events affecting the firm, significant operating and financing activities, and perhaps, prospects for the future.

2. A description of the major products or services of the company, what markets are served, where facilities are located, and a list of major subsidiary companies.

3. A narrative review of the operations for the past year. This may be broken down by segment (product line or geographic area). This review is much more in-depth than the president's letter and is designed to help the annual report user more easily interpret the financial statements by expanding on the information they contain.

4. A statement of accounting policies. There are often several alternative ways to measure assets, liabilities, revenues, and expenses; and companies may choose the particular GAAP they wish to use. The description of accounting policies can be useful for a user of financial statements, especially if financial statements of several companies using different principles are being compared. This is especially important in an international context, since the differences in accounting worldwide are even more extensive than they are domestically.

5. Notes (or footnotes) to the financial statements. These elaborate on the amounts in the financial statements. Most companies like to keep their financial statements as lean and uncluttered as possible. Extra details and disclosures that do not fit conveniently in the financial statements are then placed in the footnotes.

FINANCIAL AND NONFINANCIAL DISCLOSURE

Disclosures in financial reports are often classified as either financial or nonfinancial. *Financial* disclosures consist of those items of information quantifiable in monetary amounts (dollars, for U.S. companies). For example, companies often report one figure for inventory on the balance sheet but show in a footnote how much of that is finished goods, how much is raw materials, and so on. A company may show one amount for property in the balance sheet and reveal in a footnote how much is located in the United States, how much in Europe, and so forth. When a company signs a long-term contract obligating it to rent property for a number of years, that obligation does not fit the definition of a liability and therefore will not appear on the balance sheet. However, because cash has been committed for future years, much like the commitments that are considered liabilities, companies generally show lease obligations in footnotes. Similarly, if a company is a defendant in a lawsuit, it wants shareholders to know the amounts of potential damages it may be liable for. The case may not have progressed far enough in the courts for the defendant to know whether it will actually have to pay damages. And so, in the meantime, it reveals in a footnote the general circumstances surrounding the lawsuit. These are all types of financial disclosures seen in financial statements. For various reasons, the related monetary amounts do not appear in the financial statements themselves. They are disclosed in footnotes (or elsewhere in the annual report) to more fully inform the reader about the company's financial well-being.

Nonfinancial disclosures are either (1) narrative descriptions, facts, or opinions that do not readily lend themselves to quantification in monetary terms or (2) items of information quantified in something other than money. An example of the former is a company's mission statement. An example of the latter is data about the number of employees located in each country. (Labor *costs* per country are a financial disclosure, but *number* of employees is nonfinancial.) Nonfinancial disclosures may be just another way to express things that are already expressed monetarily in the financial statements. Most of the information that accountants provide is financial—financial statements and financial disclosures. However, not everything can be expressed monetarily, and nonfinancial disclosures can be very important, too.

SOME OBSERVATIONS ABOUT DISCLOSURE

Disclosures can also be distinguished based on whether they are required or suggested, or whether they are voluntary. While most countries *require* certain disclosures to be made by companies operating within their borders, the amount of disclosure required varies by country. Often the GAAP of a particular country will also *suggest* items to be disclosed in companies' annual reports. Many companies, though, disclose information that is neither required nor suggested; that is, some disclosures are completely *voluntary*. Disclosures that are required or suggested in one country may be voluntary in another, and vice versa.

The fact that companies sometimes disclose more than they have to suggests that they perceive some advantages in doing so. In particular, it appears that the worldwide competition for investment funds is the most important force propelling increased levels of disclosure by multinational corporations. MNCs significantly increase disclosure whenever they seek major amounts of new funds.

Disclosure can also enlarge the scope of interest in a company by expanding the annual report's audience. After all, the annual report is the major vehicle for getting people interested in what the company is doing. Chapter 1 explained how companies orient their annual report to a primary audience group—shareholders, creditors, the government, and so on. Disclosure enables the firm to maintain the primary orientation of its financial statements and provide information of interest to other parties as well. Continental European companies are especially effective and innovative in doing this.

Disclosure can overcome differences in generally accepted accounting principles. The problems associated with transnational financial reporting for financial statement users and multinational corporations are discussed in Chapters 3 and 4.

Until a worldwide harmonization of accounting practices is achieved, disclosure can be an effective mechanism for overcoming these problems.

Deciding what and what not to disclose is not always an easy decision for corporate managements to make. If they decide not to disclose an item of information, in a very real sense, they have chosen to keep something secret from financial statement users. Many things, of course, are simply irrelevant to users of financial statements—the size of the company president's waistline, for example. But for many items of information, managements must use judgment to decide on their usefulness to financial statement readers. If too much information is disclosed, a reader can easily get lost in all of the clutter (i.e., suffer from "information overload"). So managements need a way to pare down the amount of information revealed in financial statements.

Disclosure is a substantive issue, since information *revealed* can potentially affect people's decisions and actions. Unrevealed information does not have that potential. When GAAP require a disclosure, this is tantamount to saying that the information is potentially significant enough to affect decisions and, therefore, ought to be revealed. A suggested disclosure or a voluntary disclosure should be made whenever knowledge of that information has the potential to influence the decisions of financial statement users.

EXAMPLES OF DISCLOSURE

This chapter examines disclosure from an international perspective. It also illustrates certain disclosures made by European multinational corporations that are not typically made by U.S. firms. Some disclosures have a longer tradition and are better developed in Europe than in the United States. This is one area where U.S. accountants can learn from their European cousins.

What, how much, and how a company discloses supplemental information varies depending on (1) the requirements of generally accepted accounting principles, (2) the needs of users, (3) the influence of users, and (4) the philosophy of management. This chapter specifically looks at

1. Segment disclosures.
2. Financial forecast disclosures.
3. Information about shares and shareholders.
4. The value added statement.
5. Employee disclosures.
6. Environmental disclosures.

Segment Disclosures

Consolidated financial statements combine the separate financial statements of a parent company and its subsidiaries so that a single set of financial statements is issued for the entire economic entity. This subject is discussed in Chapter 6, where the argument is made that for a multinational corporation operating in a number of different countries and perhaps having several different product lines, consolidated financial statements may in fact hide some important information. If a company's continued profitability depends heavily on a certain region of the world or on a particular product, knowledge of that may be useful to shareholders, creditors, employees, and other financial statement users. After all, not all areas of the world have equally risky business environments or present equal business opportunities. Products vary in terms of risks and returns as well. Thus, in addition to consolidated financial statements, perhaps companies should provide, supplementally, more details about where and how total profits are derived.

The purpose of *disaggregated* geographic and product line disclosure is to aid the financial statement user to identify a company's *dependency* on a country, area of the world, or product line. Accounting researchers have determined that investors can improve their predictions about a company's future prospects when they are given financial information disaggregated by geographic region and "line of business" in addition to consolidated financial information.

Large U.S. multinationals are required to observe FASB Statement 131, "Disclosures about Segments of an Enterprise and Related Information." Statement 131 requires the use of a "management approach" in identifying operating segments. The statement defines an operating segment as "components of an enterprise for which separate financial information is available and evaluated regularly by the company's chief operating decision maker in allocating resources and assessing performance."[1] The FASB believes that financial statement users should be able to see the risks and opportunities of a business segment through the eyes of management.

In addition to information about products and geographic areas, Statement 131 requires that annual financial statements include certain financial and descriptive information about reportable operating segments, including:

- General information describing the activities of the segment.

- Information about segment profit and loss (including certain revenue and expense items), segment assets, and the basis of measurement.

- Reconciliations of the totals of segment revenues, profit or loss, assets, and other significant items to corresponding amounts in the balance sheet or income statement.

Exhibit 5–1 (pp. 75–76) shows how SPS Technologies complies with FASB Statement 131. Notice that SPS has four reportable segments—fasteners, specialty materials and alloys, magnetic materials, and other. The company also defines four geographic areas—the United States, England and Ireland, Brazil, and other. SPS separately discloses the following by line of business: net sales, operating earnings, total assets, depreciation and amortization, and capital additions. SPS discloses net sales and total long-lived assets by geographic area.

---

[1]Financial Accounting Standards Board. *Statement of Financial Accounting Standard No. 131: Disclosures about Segments of an Enterprise and Related Information.* Norwalk, Connecticut: FASB, June 1997.

EXHIBIT 5–1   SPS Technologies Segment Disclosure

18. Segments and Related Information

The Company adopted SFAS No. 131, "Disclosures about Segments of an Enterprise and Related Information," in 1998, which changes the way the Company reports information about its operating segments. Financial data for prior periods have been restated to conform to the 1998 presentation.

The Company's seven business groups have separate management teams that report operating results regularly, which are reviewed by the chief operating decision makers of the Company. Certain business groups have been aggregated into the same reportable segment because they have similar products and services, production processes, types of customers, and distribution methods; and their long-term financial performance is affected by similar economic conditions.

The Company has four reportable segments: Fasteners, Specialty Materials and Alloys, Magnetic Materials, and Other. The Fasteners segment consists of three business groups that produce fasteners for the aerospace, automotive, and industrial machinery markets. The Specialty Materials and Alloys segment produces specialty metals, superalloys, and ceramic cores for aerospace, industrial gas turbine, and medical applications. The Magnetic Materials segment produces magnetic materials and products used in automotive, aerospace, reprographic, computer, and advertising specialty markets. The Other segment consists of two business groups that produce structural assemblies for the aerospace market and precision consumable tools used for metal forming and cutting.

The accounting policies of the segments are the same as those described in the summary of significant accounting policies. Intersegment sales are precision tools from the Other segment sold to the Fasteners segment at the market based sales prices. The Company evaluates performance based on operating earnings of the respective segments. No single customer or group under common control represented 10% or more of the Company's net sales during 1998, 1997, and 1996.

Segments Information

	1998	1997	1996
Net Sales:			
Fasteners	$425,530	$382,505	$327,245
Specialty Materials & Alloys	112,782	82,777	66,724
Magnetic Materials	140,409	110,971	84,502
Other	45,729	20,521	14,737
Intersegment	(7,845)	(8,158)	(7,305)
Net Sales	$716,605	$588,616	$485,903
Operating earnings:			
Fasteners	$ 52,238	$ 41,104	$ 26,645
Specialty Materials & Alloys	15,132	10,986	8,603
Magnetic Materials	17,834	14,394	10,978
Other	4,530	1,294	352
Unallocated Corporate Costs	(10,400)	(9,700)	(8,400)
Operating earnings	$ 79,334	$ 58,078	$ 38,178

EXHIBIT 5–1 *(Concluded)*

Segments Information—*Cont.*

	1998	1997	1996
Total assets:			
Fasteners	$317,366	$280,958	$285,672
Specialty Materials & Alloys	70,838	45,578	32,448
Magnetic Materials	118,097	124,762	99,985
Other	100,934	20,750	9,895
Total assets	$607,235	$472,048	$428,000

Depreciation and Amortization and Capital Additions:

	Depreciation and Amortization			Capital Additions		
	1998	1997	1996	1998	1997	1996
Fasteners	$17,389	$14,515	$12,724	$19,445	$24,445	$20,829
Specialty Materials & Alloys	2,243	1,418	953	6,082	4,966	2,339
Magnetic Materials	7,321	5,950	4,216	3,482	7,224	3,972
Other	2,376	1,200	1,009	3,075	875	1,080
Total	$29,329	$23,083	$18,902	$32,084	$37,510	$28,220

Geographic Areas

	1998	1997	1996
Net sales:			
United States	$517,693	$413,206	$335,489
England and Ireland	145,560	111,105	89,935
Brazil	22,627	27,399	24,955
Other	30,725	36,906	35,524
Net sales	$716,605	$588,616	$485,903
Long-lived assets:			
United States	$200,305	$155,331	$113,208
England and Ireland	109,827	59,624	49,700
Brazil	12,660	14,570	14,356
Other	12,503	15,635	18,960
Total long-lived assets	$335,295	$245,160	$196,224

The Other geographic areas consist principally of Australia, Canada, China, Japan, Mexico, and Singapore. For geographic area disclosure purposes, the Company considers investments in affiliates, property, plant and equipment and other assets, as disclosed in the Consolidated Balance Sheets, to be long-lived assets.

Certain disaggregated disclosures by the British firm Cadbury Schweppes are reproduced in Exhibit 5–2 (pp. 77–80). Cadbury Schweppes uses a matrix format to disclose sales, trading profit, operating assets, and trading margin by product line and geographic area. The company defines two product lines—beverages and confectionary (candies). It also defines five geographic regions—the United Kingdom, (Continental) Europe, the Americas, the Pacific Rim, and Africa & Others. Cadbury Schweppes also provides an in-depth analysis of its operations by product line (not reproduced here). A matrix presentation provides more detail than separate product line and geographic area disclosures. However, the approach is not very common.

EXHIBIT 5–2 Cadbury Schweppes Segmental Analysis (Segmental Analysis for the 52 weeks ended 2 January 1999 (Note 1)

1998	Total £m	United Kingdom £m	Europe £m	Americas £m	Pacific Rim £m	Africa and Others £m
Sales						
Beverages	1,937	55	346	1,250	201	85
Confectionery	2,169	948	453	265	304	199
	4,106	1,003	799	1,515	505	284
Trading Profit (b)						
Beverages	362	(12)	38	301	21	14
Confectionery	280	134	23	43	58	22
	642	122	61	344	79	36
Operating Assets						
Beverages	260	(38)	59	172	47	20
Confectionery	1,002	366	218	107	178	133
	1,262	328	277	279	225	153
Trading Margin (b)	%	%	%	%	%	%
Beverages	18.7	(21.8)	11.0	24.1	10.4	16.5
Confectionery	12.9	14.1	5.1	16.2	19.1	11.1
	15.6	12.2	7.6	22.7	15.6	12.7

(a) In 1997, United Kingdom beverages includes sales and trading profit of £47m and £4m relating to discontinued operations

(b) Excluding major restructuring costs of £14m in 1998 and £20m in 1997, and Exceptional items of £68m in 1998 (see Note 3)

Trading profit for beverages and confectionery in the United Kingdom is stated after deducting corporate costs that have been allocated equally. Sales and trading profit by destination and origin are not materially different.

EXHIBIT 5–2 *(Continued)*

1997	Total £m	United Kingdom £m	Europe £m	Americas £m	Pacific Rim £m	Africa and Others £m
Sales (a)						
Beverages	2,000	114	361	1,211	222	92
Confectionery	2,220	955	427	267	351	220
	4,220	1,069	788	1,478	573	312
Trading Profit (a)(b)						
Beverages	346	—	36	277	19	14
Confectionery	282	132	23	41	59	27
	628	132	59	318	78	41
Operating Assets						
Beverages	273	(39)	63	168	55	26
Confectionery	1,041	353	243	106	187	152
	1,314	314	306	274	242	178
Trading Margin (b)	%	%	%	%	%	%
Beverages	17.3	—	10.0	22.9	8.6	15.2
Confectionery	12.7	13.8	5.4	15.4	16.8	12.3
	14.9	12.3	7.5	21.5	13.6	13.1

(a) In 1997, United Kingdom beverages includes sales and trading profit of £47m and £4m relating to discontinued operations

(b) Excluding major restructuring costs of £14m in 1998 and £20m in 1997, and Exceptional items of £68m in 1998 (see Note 3)

Trading profit for beverages and confectionery in the United Kingdom is stated after deducting corporate costs that have been allocated equally. Sales and trading profit by destination and origin are not materially different.

Presenting disaggregated data is now common among large multinational corporations. Several countries require it, the International Accounting Standards Committee has issued (revised) *Standard 14*, "Segment Reporting," the European Union's Fourth directive requires disclosure of sales by line of business and by geographic segment, and both the United Nations and the Organization for Economic Cooperation and Development (discussed in Chapter 3) suggest such disclosures by multinationals.

There is a wide variety in the segment disclosure practices of multinationals throughout the world. Exhibit 5–3 (p.81) provides a comparison across the European Union countries of corporate disclosure by line of business segment and by

EXHIBIT 5–2   *(Continued)*

1996	Total £m	United Kingdom £m	Europe £m	Americas £m	Pacific Rim £m	Africa and Others £m
Sales (a)						
Beverages	2,875	952	415	1,194	228	86
Confectionery	2,240	941	464	262	386	187
	5,115	1,893	879	1,456	614	273
Trading Profit (a)(b)						
Beverages	445	113	27	271	20	14
Confectionery	267	118	28	33	67	21
	712	231	55	304	87	35
Operating Assets (a)						
Beverages	469	203	77	95	74	20
Confectionery	1,028	354	251	95	230	98
	1,497	557	328	190	304	118
Trading Margin (b)	%	%	%	%	%	%
Beverages	15.5	11.9	6.5	22.7	8.8	16.3
Confectionery	11.9	12.5	6.0	12.6	17.4	11.2
	13.9	12.2	6.3	20.9	14.2	12.8

(a) United Kingdom beverages includes sales and trading profit and operating assets of £921m and £124m and £214m, respectively, relating to discontinued operations

(b) Excluding major restructuring costs of £41m (see Note 3)

Trading profit for beverages and confectionery in the United Kingdom is stated after deducting corporate costs which have been allocated equally. Sales and trading profit by destination and origin are not materially different.

geographic segment. The majority of all firms disclose sales by line of business and geographic segments as required by the European Union's Fourth Directive. But when it comes to reporting segment information on profits and assets, only firms from the United Kingdom score high.

Clearly, defining product lines is easier than defining meaningful geographic segments. Countries and regions vary in terms of (1) stage of development, (2) political risk, (3) currency strength, (4) inflation levels, and (5) economic stability. The risks associated with these variables somehow need to be conveyed. This represents a significant challenge for accountants.

EXHIBIT 5–2   *(Concluded)*

Supplementary Reportable Segment Information

	1998 £m	1997 £m	1996 £m
Depreciation and amortisation			
Beverages	42	41	85
Confectionery	163	104	98
	205	145	183
Capital Expenditure			
Beverages	54	74	96
Confectionery	108	135	153
	162	209	249
Identifiable Assets			
Beverages	2,633	2,637	2,750
Confectionery	1,960	2,130	1,757
	4,593	4,767	4,507

Corporate assets have been allocated equally to each segment.

Supplementary Geographical Information

	Sales			Fixed Assets	
	1998 £m	1997 £m	1996 £m	1998 £m	1997 £m
UK	1,003	1,069	1,893	444	431
US	1,100	1,055	993	1,595	1,524
Australia	402	450	470	154	167
All others	1,601	1,646	1,759	711	747
	4,106	4,220	5,115	2,904	2,869

Financial Forecast Disclosures

Given that a primary concern of investors is assessing a company's future profitability and cash flows, it is reasonable to ask whether companies provide their own internal forecasts of such financial information. Financial forecasts would seem to be relevant information for investors. In practice, few MNCs provide them. One reason is that forecasts can be unreliable because they incorporate (often highly) subjective estimates of uncertain future events. In addition, there can be legal repercussions for managements if the forecasts are not met. In

EXHIBIT 5–3   European Union Segment Disclosure

LOB Segments

	Belgium	Denmark	France	Germany	Ireland	Netherlands	United Kingdom	Other	Overall
(n =	18	24	30	29	22	28	29	25	205)
	%	%	%	%	%	%	%	%	%
Sales	100.0	83.3	93.3	100.0	86.4	96.4	96.6	96.0	94.1
Profits	38.9	33.3	53.3	20.7	36.4	35.7	93.1	24.0	42.9
Assets	11.1	41.7	30.0	0.0	31.8	17.9	100.0	24.0	33.2
Employees	27.8	50.0	36.7	58.6	31.8	35.7	41.4	32.0	40.0
Capital Expenditure	16.7	8.3	33.3	37.9	0.0	21.4	13.8	24.0	20.5
Other[a]	27.8	33.3	80.0	69.0	0.0	25.0	6.9	68.0	40.5
Average items per firm	2.2	2.5	3.3	2.9	1.9	2.3	3.5	2.7	2.7

GEOG Segments

	Belgium	Denmark	France	Germany	Ireland	Netherlands	United Kingdom	Other	Overall
(n =	19	24	30	29	25	30	29	27	213)
	%	%	%	%	%	%	%	%	%
Sales	79.0	95.8	100.0	100.0	80.0	100.0	100.0	88.9	93.9
Profits	5.3	8.3	46.7	10.3	36.0	16.7	89.7	11.1	29.6
Assets	5.3	8.3	46.7	0.0	28.0	16.7	96.6	11.1	28.2
Employees	31.6	33.3	46.7	27.6	16.0	43.3	24.1	11.1	29.6
Capital Expenditure	5.3	0.0	23.3	10.3	0.0	13.3	10.3	7.4	9.4
Other	10.5	16.7	60.0	20.7	28.0	13.3	65.5	29.6	31.9
Average items per firm	1.4	1.6	3.2	1.7	1.9	2.0	3.9	1.6	2.2

Note: [a]The other category contains a variety of items including gross profit, sales orders, research & development, cash flows, investments, inventory, fixed assets, depreciation, and production costs.

n = number of companies responding

SOURCE: Reprinted from *Journal of International Accounting, Auditing, & Taxation*, vol. 5, no. 1, D. Herrmann and W. Thomas, "Segment Reporting in the European Union: Analyzing the Effects of Country, Size, Industry, and Exchange Listing," p. 9, Copyright 1996, with permission from Elsevier Science.

litigious countries such as the United States, the potential for lawsuits is a major deterrent to providing financial forecasts.

Though unusual by international norms, some forecast disclosures can be observed, notably by some larger Danish and Swedish MNCs. For example, the 1998 annual report of J. Lauritzen Holding Group, the Danish shipping, transport, and industrial products company, forecasts the following for 1999:

> 1999 is expected to show significant growth in the result on ordinary activities. Overall, a net result of approximately DKK 1.1 billion is anticipated.

Information about Shares and Shareholders

A number of continental European companies disclose rather extensive information about their shares and shareholders. Exhibit 5–4 (pp. 83–86) is an example of such a disclosure provided by the Finnish paper and board machinery company Valmet in its annual report. Share information disclosed by - Valmet includes the following: (1) discussion of a variety of issues that impact Valmet stock, (2) share data, (3) monthly trading range and turnover of Valmet shares on the Helsinki exchange, (4) Valmet's American Depository Share data, (5) shareholders by category, and (6) distribution of Valmet shareholders, including the identity and number of shares owned by its 16 largest shareholders.

What is the value of such information? It is aimed primarily at current and prospective shareholders. Past trend data can be useful in predicting future patterns, and it is also useful when making comparisons with the trends of other companies. Shares are more marketable when they are traded on several exchanges and when the volume of trading is high. Widely scattered ownership tends to provide ready sales opportunities when present shareholders wish to dispose of some or all of their share holdings. Ownership concentration also indicates the locus of corporate control. On the other hand, dispersed ownership normally means that the company is controlled by shareholders and their agents, the company's management team. On the other hand, a concentrated ownership suggests that power is exerted by a more narrowly defined group. Management may be constrained if a large block of shares is owned by relatively few individuals or groups, and other shareholders may have relatively less influence in such situations. The identities of the largest shareholders might also be of interest to current and potential shareholders for the same reason.

Information such as that in Exhibit 5–4 is provided voluntarily. There are no standards, such as from the organizations discussed in Chapter 3, that require companies to provide information about shares and shareholders. Although the practice seems to be growing, it is still not very widespread.

The Value Added Statement

The value added statement originated in Europe and is now occasionally provided by companies from outside Europe (e.g., Australia and South Africa). To our knowledge, no country's GAAP require value added statements. Thus, they are provided on a completely voluntary basis.

The statement produced by the South African firm Bolton Footwear is reproduced in Exhibit 5–5 (p. 87). This statement shows that Bolton added wealth of R85,910 million to the world economy in 1998. This contribution went to the following groups:

1. Employees, in the form of salaries, pension, and so forth.
2. Providers of capital, in the form of dividends to shareholders and interest to creditors.

EXHIBIT 5–4   Valmet, Information about Shares and Shareholders

Valmet Corporation's share capital totals FIM 851 million. According to Valmet's Articles of Association, there is one series of shares. The total number of shares issued and outstanding is 78,100,000. No shareholder can vote with more than 80 percent of the total votes represented at the General Meeting. According to the Corporation's Articles of Association, a shareholder whose total shareholding or voting rights reach or exceed $33^1/_3$ percent or 50 percent, shall, upon demand, acquire the shares held by other shareholders at a price specified in the Articles.

The Corporation's shares have been quoted on the Helsinki Exchanges since 1988. The shares have been joined to the book entry securities system, in which shareholdings are registered in book entry accounts held by various book entry registrars. Foreign shareholders may alternatively register their shares in nominee accounts administered by a custodian. Nominee-registered shares have no voting rights. Valmet's American Depository Shares (ADS), representing two ordinary shares each, have been listed on the New York Stock Exchange since 1996 and traded under a sticker VA.NYSE.

During 1998, 44.6 million Valmet shares were traded on the Helsinki Exchanges at an average price per share of FIM 77.29. The number of ADSs traded on the New York Stock Exchange was 1.0 million, and the average price was USD 30.74 per ADS.

On November 17, 1998, the Boards of Directors of Rauma and Valmet announced a plan, under which Rauma and Valmet will merge to create a new combined company. In the merger each outstanding share of Rauma will be converted into 1.08917 shares of Valmet-Rauma, and each share of Valmet will be converted into one share of Valmet-Rauma. Since November 17, 1998, the share prices of Valmet Corporation and Rauma Corporation have moved in relation to each other in accordance with the proposed conversion ratio.

The 1994 Annual General Meeting approved an issue of bonds with warrants, valued at FIM 500,000, to members of Valmet Corporation's senior management. The bonds are valid for five years, carrying an interest rate of 5 percent and an issue price of 100 percent. The warrants entitle the holders to subscribe to a maximum of 1,000,000 shares from December 1, 1998, to January 31, 2001, at a subscription price of FIM 60.00. The bonds with warrants were completely subscribed. In connection with the approval of Valmet-Rauma's merger plan on November 17, 1998, the Board of Directors of Valmet determined that warrant holders would be eligible to subscribe for Valmet shares during the period from December 1, 1998, to May 31, 1999, and for Valmet-Rauma shares from the completion of the merger until January 31, 2001, at the original subscription price and in accordance with the original terms of warrants. The subscription rights of warrants had not been used by February 16, 1999.

The 1998 Annual General Meeting approved an issue of two series of warrants to persons belonging to the management of the Group and certain other key persons. The warrants entitle the holders to subscribe to an aggregate of 2,000,000 shares in the Company (1,000,000 shares in each series). The subscription period for the new shares will commence on April 1, 2001, for the first series, entitling holders to subscribe for new shares of Valmet at a price of FIM 108 per share, and on April 1, 2003, for the second series, entitling the holders to subscribe for new shares of Valmet at a price of FIM 113 per share. The subscription period for both series will close on March 31, 2005. The share

---

EXHIBIT 5–4 *(Continued)*

Share Data	1994	1995	1996	1997	*1998*
Share capital, Dec 31, MFIM	851	851	851	851	**851**
Number of shares					
Number of shares, Dec. 31	85 101 430	85 101 430	78 100 000	78 100 000	**78 100 000**
Average number of shares	79 079 512	85 101 430	81 130 756	78 100 000	**78 100 000**
Trading volume, Helsinki Exchanges	26 552 340	24 751 770	44 980 204	53 648 851	**44 584 487**
Share issues, MFIM					
Increase in share capital	140				
Surplus over nominal value	505				
Number of shares redeemed and cancelled	—	—	7 001 430	—	**—**
Dividend, MFIM	43	149	234	273	**273**[1]
Dividend / share, FIM	0.50	1.75	3.00	3.50	**3.50**[1]
Dividend yield, %	1.1	3.2	3.7	4.7	**5.1**
Earnings / share, FIM	2.50	6.74	10.26	10.08	**8.64**
P/E ratio	18.02	8.09	7.89	7.46	**7.87**
Cash flow / share, FIM	8.22	11.35	15.88	15.32	**15.25**
Equity / share, FIM	29.45	36.03	41.57	49.85	**54.06**
Nominal value, FIM	10	10	10	10	**10**
Highest quotation, FIM	64.50	72.50	83.50	98.00	**102.00**
Lowest quotation, FIM	34.50	39.50	52.00	69.00	**48.00**
Quotation, Dec 31, FIM	45.00	54.50	81.00	75.20	**68.00**
Market value of shares, Dec 31, FIM millions	3 830	4 638	6 326	5 873	**5 311**

[1]Proposal by the Board of Directors
The two-for-one share split has been taken into account in the table above for all years presented.

---

subscription price for both series will be adjusted by dividends distributed after May 1, 1998, and before the date of subscription. In connection with the approval of Valmet-Rauma's merger plan on November 17, 1998, the Board of Directors of Valmet determined that warrant holders would also be eligible to subscribe for Valmet shares during the period from April 1, 1999, to May 31, 1999. Following completion of the merger, the options will entitle holders to subscribe for shares of Valmet-Rauma at the original subscription price and in accordance with the original terms of options.

No other bonds with warrants or convertible bonds have been outstanding during 1998. Valmet Corporation does not currently have an authorization to issue shares or warrants, or to buy back its own shares.

EXHIBIT 5–4   *(Continued)*

Monthly Trading Range of Valmet Shares on the Helsinki Exchanges

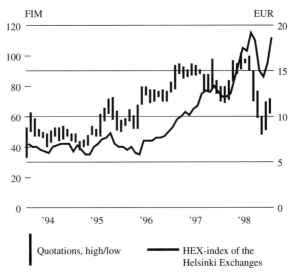

Quotations, high/low   ━━━ HEX-index of the Helsinki Exchanges

Monthly Turnover of Shares on the Helsinki Exchanges, 1,000 Shares

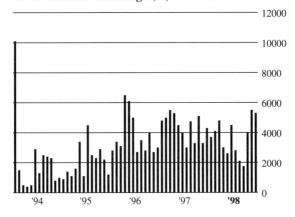

ADS data (Each ADS represents two shares)	1997	1998
Trading volume, New York Stock Exchange	521 522	**928 034**
Earnings/ADS, USD	3.70	**3.41**
Highest quotation, USD	38.50	**36.31**
Lowest quotation, USD	26.50	**18.88**
Quotation, Dec 31, USD	27.50	**26.31**

EXHIBIT 5–4   *(Concluded)*

Shareholders by category Dec. 31, 1998	Number of Shareholders	% of Shareholders	% of Shares
Companies	366	3.7	1.3
Financial institutions and insurance companies	87	0.9	19.5
Public institutions	12	0.1	23.0
Foundations and associations	229	2.3	4.5
Private individuals	9 260	92.6	4.0
Foreign shareholders	44	0.4	0.1
Registered shareholders, total	9 998	100.0	52.4
Nominee registered			47.6
Shares not converted into book entries			0.0
Shareholdings, total			100.0

Shareholders Dec. 31, 1998	Number of Shareholders	Number of Shareholders	% of Shares
The Finnish Government		15 695 287	20.1
Ilmarinen Mutual Insurance Company		3 192 400	4.1
Varma-Sampo Mutual Pension Insurance Company		2 507 032	3.2
The Local Government Pensions Institution		1 709 300	2.2
Pohjola Life Assurance Company Ltd.		1 061 500	1.4
Industrial Insurance Company Ltd.		975 000	1.2
Pohjola Non-Life Insurance Company Ltd.		865 000	1.1
Suomi Mutual Life Assurance Company		680 000	0.9
Sampo Assurance Company plc		500 000	0.6
Valmet Corporation Personnel Fund		466 700	0.6
Mutual Insurance Company Pension-Fennia		456 068	0.6
Kaleva Mutual Insurance Company		434 000	0.6
Tapiola General Mutual Insurance Company		422 200	0.5
Social Insurance Institution		372 200	0.5
Sampo Enterprise Insurance Company Limited		370 000	0.5
Sampo Life Insurance Company Limited		360 000	0.5
	16	30 066 687	38.6
Other shareholders, shares / shareholder			
100 001 – 359 999	18	3 236 227	4.1
10 001 – 100 000	103	3 408 525	4.4
5 001 – 10 000	83	611 138	0.8
1 001 – 5 000	823	1 547 024	2.0
501 – 1 000	978	744 850	0.9
101 – 500	4 814	1 085 929	1.4
1 – 100	3 163	176 168	0.2
Nominee registered		37 199 052	47.6
Shares not converted into book entries		24 400	0.0
Total	9 998	78 100 000	100.0

Members of the Company Board of Directors own a total of 5,390 shares, that is 0.007 percent of the total votes carried by all stock. Additionally they hold warrants to subscribe for up to 0.31 percent of the outstanding shares

EXHIBIT 5–5   Bolton Footwear, Value Added Statement

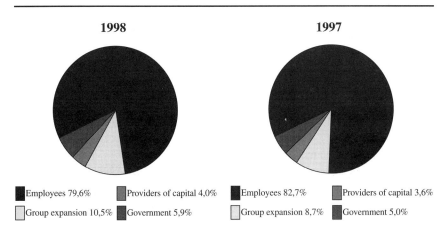

| *At 28 February 1998* | *1998* | | *1997* | |
	R'000	*%*	*R'000*	*%*
Value Added				
Turnover	264 596	100,0	239 305	100,0
Cost of materials and services	180 051	68,0	171 079	71,5
Value added	84 545	32,0	68 226	28,5
Interest received	1 365		—	
Total wealth created	85 910		68 226	
Value Distributed				
Compensation to employees	68 407	79,6	56 395	82,7
Reward to providers of capital:	3 467	4,0	2 509	3,6
—Dividends to shareholders	2 700	3,1	1 600	2,3
—Interest on borrowings	—	—	187	0,3
—Lease payments on premises and machinery	767	0,9	722	1,0
Charges by government and local authorities	5 093	5,9	3 385	5,0
—Direct tax on profits	3 892	4,5	2 401	3,5
—Tax on distribution of profits to shareholders	337	0,4	187	0,3
—Regional Services Council levy	596	0,7	542	0,8
—Municipal rates and taxes	268	0,3	255	0,4
Retained for Reinvestment				
Depreciation	2 985	3,5	2 678	4,0
Retained profit	5 958	7,0	3 259	4,7
	85 910	100,0	68 226	100,0
Number of employees at year-end	2 161		1 983	

3. Governments, in the form of taxes.

4. Bolton itself—amounts reinvested in the business.

The value added statement presents the view that a corporation is a provider of wealth to society—that its presence is a positive force. Because the corporation exists, people are employed, governments receive more taxes, and investors and creditors are rewarded for risking their funds in the business. The value added statement reflects the philosophy that a business enterprise should, and actually *does,* do more than just make a profit. It is consistent with the notion that creating employment and making other contributions to society at large are also legitimate objectives of business. This is not the prevailing attitude in the United States, but it is in most other countries of the world. One can see that the environmental variables discussed in Chapter 1 affect not only measurement practices but also disclosure practices.

Employee Disclosures

Exhibit 5–6 (pp. 88–96) is reproduced from the annual report of the Greek aluminum company ALUMINIUM DE GRECE. Notice that Exhibit 5–6 shows information about age, salaries, training, and absenteeism. Employee disclosures reflect the viewpoint that a company's continued success depends in part on its employees, or human resources. Exhibit 5–6 also demonstrates the influence of organized labor in Europe, where it is relatively more powerful than in the United States.

EXHIBIT 5–6   ALUMINIUM DE GRECE, Employee Disclosures

Personnel

ALUMINIUM DE GRECE has significantly increased its competitivity on a world-wide scale.

This development was made possible by adapting organisation procedures and by raising skill levels, accompanied by an investment plan.

One result of this policy is the reduction of the workforce, the necessity for which has been recognised by all employees.

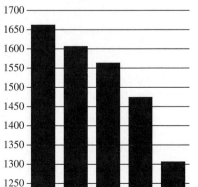

Annual Trend of Average Workforce

EXHIBIT 5–6 *(Continued)*

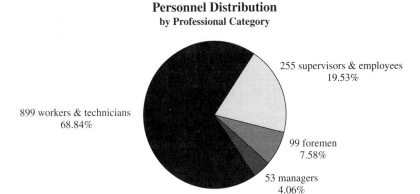

Personnel Distribution
by Professional Category

255 supervisors & employees
19.53%

899 workers & technicians
68.84%

99 foremen
7.58%

53 managers
4.06%

Average workforce in 1998 - 1306 agents

Personnel turnover

The turnover of personnel in 1998 was 10%.

This percentage is near the average for the last five years, which was significantly influenced by the programme for voluntary early retirement, proposed to personnel in 1997.

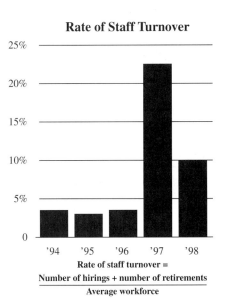

Rate of Staff Turnover

Rate of staff turnover =

$$\frac{\text{Number of hirings + number of retirements}}{\text{Average workforce}}$$

EXHIBIT 5–6   *(Continued)*

Retirements by Cause

	1994	1995	1996	1997	1998
Pension	20	19	26	19	6
Early Retirement	0	0	0	283	22
Resignation	20	7	11	7	29
Other	8	12	8	10	6
Total	**48**	**38**	**45**	**319**	**63**

Hirings

	1994	1995	1996	1997	1998
Number of hirings	13	11	10	10	70

Age—Seniority

Distribution of personnel by age and seniority is following a positive course.

The course of average seniority and age was reversed, as these showed lower levels for the first time.

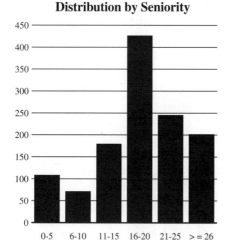

Distribution by Seniority

Average seniority at December 31, 1998: 18.06 years

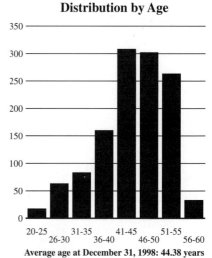

Distribution by Age

Average age at December 31, 1998: 44.38 years

EXHIBIT 5–6   *(Continued)*

Absenteeism

Absenteeism, not including annual leave days, was 3.6% of work days for 1998. This is the lowest level recorded, at least in the last decade.

It includes:

- 0.27% due to labour accidents, which is higher than in 1997. The Company is intensifying its efforts, in the framework of coordinated action, to return this index to the downward trend of previous years.
- 2.70% due to sickness, maternity and union activity, and
- 0.60% leave without pay, due to the Union of Workers and Company Employees participation in national strikes called by higher union organisations (General Confederation of Greek Workers, POEM).

There were no absences in 1998 caused by strikes on industrial relations issues.

Absenteeism by Cause

Total work days	**416,934**	**410,754**	**399,463**	**381,348**	**336,175**
Annual leave days	**45,974**	**46,122**	**45,317**	**44,570**	**35,232**
	11.0%	11.2%	11.3%	11.7%	10.48%
Days lost because of accidents	712	720	867	493	891
Days lost through illness	13,550	12,857	12,859	12,058	8,928
Absence with pay	1,164	1,020	1,136	984	406
Absence without pay	1,311	6,335	1,892	10,043	1,974
Total days of leave	**16,737**	**20,932**	**16,754**	**23,578**	**12,199**
	4.0%	5.1%	4.2%	6.2%	3.6%

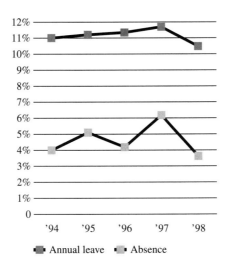

■ Annual leave   ■ Absence

EXHIBIT 5–6   *(Continued)*

Personnel—related expenses

Personnel-related expenses in 1998 amounted to GRD 21.052 billion.

They comprised gross pretax pay, Social Security contributions and other nonsalary benefits (severance pay, supplementary pension, insurance, and housing subsidies for employees).

Distribution of Personnel Expenses

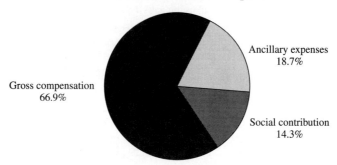

Total expenses = GRD 21.052 billion

Growth of Personnel — Related Expenses and Number of Personnel

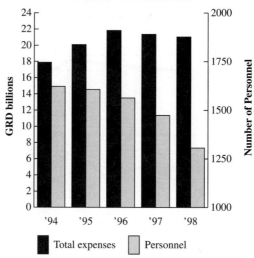

EXHIBIT 5–6   *(Continued)*

Remuneration trends for employees

The average annual gross pay per employee for 1998 was over GRD 10 million.

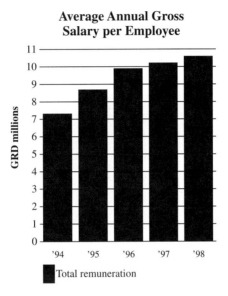

**Average Annual Gross
Salary per Employee**

■ Total remuneration

In 1998, there was no average annual gross pay under GRD 4.8 million for a regular attendance.

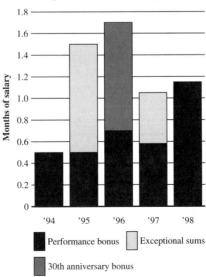

**Performance Bonus — Exceptional
Sums Expressed as Monthly Salaries**

■ Performance bonus   □ Exceptional sums

■ 30th anniversary bonus

EXHIBIT 5–6   *(Continued)*

Wages and inflation

Over the past five years, the annual increase in gross pay for all employees at ALU-MINIUM DE GRECE, excluding the variable element of profit-sharing bonus, has been above average inflation levels.

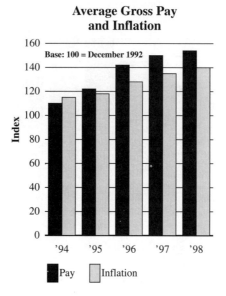

**Average Gross Pay
and Inflation**

Range of annual average remuneration

The ratio of managerial personnel remuneration to worker pay (excluding the variable element of profit-sharing bonus) was slightly over 2.5 : 1.

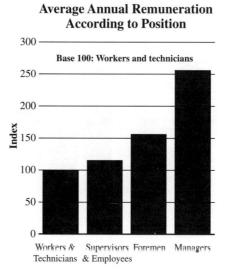

**Average Annual Remuneration
According to Position**

EXHIBIT 5–6   *(Continued)*

Occupational safety

In 1998 there was a serious slow-down in the downward trend of the frequency and severity indices of accidents, relative to short-term aims.

Even though these indices have dropped by more than half over the last decade, the Company maintains its aim to place itself rapidly in this area among the best in an international level.

Occupational Safety Indices

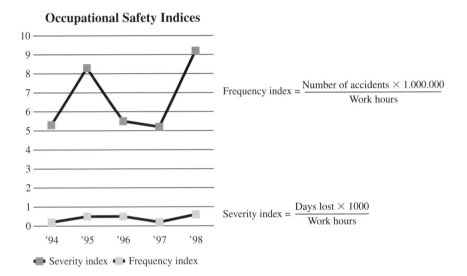

$$\text{Frequency index} = \frac{\text{Number of accidents} \times 1.000.000}{\text{Work hours}}$$

$$\text{Severity index} = \frac{\text{Days lost} \times 1000}{\text{Work hours}}$$

■ Severity index ■ Frequency index

Health and medical assistance

The Company's medical service provides regular check-ups for its personnel and first aid, on a 24-hour basis, in case of accidents or other emergencies.

Number of periodic check-ups of personnel	1,216
Number of medical examinations at hiring	122
Number of working conditions inspections	30
Number of people employed at the dispensary	7
Cost of dispensary's operation (in GRD million)	143
Cost of social worker and IKA 24-hour service (in GRD million)	31

EXHIBIT 5–6   *(Concluded)*

Training

In 1998, more than 50% of the personnel participated in general or job-related training programmes, aimed at improving professional competence and increasing learning.

	Expenses (in GRD million)	*Hours*
Cost of training dept. and general expenses	208.4	
Remuneration of employees	351.3	
Hours of on-the-job training		52,966
Hours of outside training programmes		41,061
Total training	**559.7***	**94,027**
% training expenses / total remuneration	**3.98%**	

*Total sum of rebates (through training programmes etc.) has not be detracted from training cost. This sum was GRD 54.5 million for 1998.

This type of disclosure developed in Europe and is now finding its way into the annual reports of U.S. companies. For example, Exhibit 5–7 is the employee disclosure of Ford Motor Company. It includes information about the number of employees by geographic area and the number of minority group members and women employed.

EXHIBIT 5–7   Ford Motor Company, Employee Disclosure

Employment and Payroll Data

In 1998, average worldwide employment decreased 5.1% reflecting divestiture of The Associates, offset partially by increased employment at Hertz. Worldwide payrolls were $16.9 billion in 1998, a 2.0% decrease from 1997.

Average employment by geographic area, compared with 1997, was:

	1998	*1997*
United States	173,899	189,787
Europe	105,351	104,014
Other	65,925	70,091
Total	345,175	363,892

Note: The Associates employment included above was 21,161 in 1997.

EXHIBIT 5–7   *(Concluded)*

U.S. Employment of Minority-Group Personnel and Women at Year-End*

	In United States		Minorities		Women	
	1998	*1997*	*1998*	*1997*	*1998*	*1997*
Hourly employees	**100,760**	103,569	**25.2%**	25.0%	**15.8%**	15.5%
Salaried employees	**53,309**	53,305	**16.4%**	15.7%	**26.5%**	26.0%
Total	**154,069**	156,874	**22.2%**	21.8%	**19.5%**	19.1%

*Includes Ford Motor Company and Ford Credit Company.

U.S. Representation of Minority-Group Members and Women in EEO-1 Job Categories at Year-End[a]

Job Categories[b]	African-Americans		Hispanic-Americans		Other Minorities[c]		Women	
	1998	*1997*	*1998*	*1997*	*1998*	*1997*	*1998*	*1997*
Officials and Managers	**9.0%**	8.7%	**1.8%**	1.7%	**2.8%**	2.4%	**11.8%**	10.4%
Professionals	**8.1%**	7.9%	**2.5%**	2.4%	**6.5%**	6.1%	**25.2%**	24.9%
Technicians	**7.3%**	7.1%	**2.1%**	2.0%	**2.2%**	2.1%	**14.1%**	14.2%
Office and Clerical	**18.1%**	17.5%	**4.9%**	4.6%	**1.2%**	1.1%	**48.9%**	47.4%
Craft Workers (skilled)	**8.4%**	8.9%	**1.3%**	1.2%	**0.7%**	0.6%	**2.4%**	2.5%
Operatives (semiskilled)	**25.7%**	25.6%	**2.8%**	2.7%	**0.8%**	0.8%	**20.5%**	20.0%
Laborers (nonskilled)	**30.8%**	31.5%	**2.7%**	2.3%	**0.9%**	0.7%	**11.8%**	10.7%
Service Workers	**31.5%**	29.7%	**1.9%**	2.0%	**0.1%**	0.5%	**9.3%**	15.2%
Percentage of Work Force	**17.4%**	17.3%	**2.5%**	2.5%	**2.2%**	2.0%	**19.5%**	19.1%

[a]Includes Ford Motor Company and Ford Motor Credit Company only.
[b]Excludes sales workers (retail), a job category that is not applicable to Ford.
[c]Includes Asian-American, Pacific Islanders, American Indians, or Alaskan Natives only.

Environmental Disclosures

Do you find yourself interested in vehicle emissions, protecting the ozone layer, hazardous waste incinerators, or the movement of waste? Then, you are interested in environmental safety and protection issues or *green* accounting, as it is sometimes referred to. The appropriate reporting of environmental costs and concerns is a major issue for public corporations throughout the world. According to a 1996 study done by KPMG in Sweden, an international public accounting firm, since 1993 the percentage of top 100 companies in 12 leading industrial nations that mention the environment in annual reports has almost doubled to 69 percent.[2] And 23 percent now produce a separate environmental report, compared with 13 percent in 1993. Most of these disclosures are still voluntary and nonfinancial in nature with only 18 percent of the companies in the study including environmental costs in the financial statements or the notes and/or discussing their financial policies for calculating these costs.

Exhibit 5–8 on safety and environmental protection is reproduced from the 1998 annual report of the Swiss conglomerate, Roche. Notice that Roche does report actual costs for safety and environmental protection expenditures (a financial disclosure). Other information is presented in nonfinancial prose. The paragraph on sustainable development is particularly noteworthy in that Roche makes it clear that to be financially successful, a company must be environmentally and socially responsible!

---

[2]P. Rogerson, "Greening the Global Village," *The Corporate Accountant,* November 1996, p. VIII.

EXHIBIT 5–8   Roche, Environmental Disclosures

Safety and Environmental Protection

Expenditure on safety and environmental protection in the Roche Group amounted to over 2 percent of sales. Major capital investment projects included final work on the wastewater treatment facility at the Dalry site (Scotland) and on new air emission controls in Boulder (Colorado). A substantial investment was also made for upgraded sludge dewatering at the Sisseln site (Switzerland), which resulted in a significant decrease in power consumption.

Safety and environmental protection expenditure
in millions of CHF (Swiss francs)

	1998	1997
Investment	229	264
Operating costs	363	372
Total expenditures	592	636

Accidents and incidents

As in previous years, there were no major incidents with wider repercussions. Throughout the Group the rate of occupational accidents remained at the previous year's low level and thus significantly below the average for the chemical industry as a whole. This positive trend, which has continued for many years, is due in no small part to rigorous training and continuing education, regular risk analyses and safety and environmental protection audits.

Environmental protection

The positive trend seen in previous years also continued in the environmental protection area. Despite a somewhat higher production output, energy consumption remained virtually constant. Emissions of volatile organic compounds (VOCs)

EXHIBIT 5–8   *(Concluded)*

continued to decline on average, although there were fluctuations from site to site as a result of changing production volumes. At the Belvidere site in the United States, emissions were reduced dramatically through replacement of a diesel power plant with a gas turbine-combined power and heat unit.

Total chemical waste levels also remained almost constant in comparison with 1997, despite the slight rise in production volumes. Since September the gypsum generated at Citrique Belge as a by-product of citric acid manufacture has been reprocessed for use in other industries, thus eliminating the need for land-fill disposal.

The programme under which substitutes are found for substances that contribute to destruction of the ozone layer was vigorously continued. As part of this programme a substantial amount of halon was removed from firefighting systems at our Sisseln plant and properly disposed of.

Audits

The safety and environmental protection audits carried out regularly in all Group companies since 1980 are an important element in maintaining high standards in these areas. The main focus in 1998 was the integration of Boehringer Mannheim. A previous due diligence review had already indicated that safety and environmental protection standards at the former Boehringer Mannheim plants are high, a finding the Roche audits have confirmed. A total of 35 safety and environmental audits were conducted in 22 countries during the year under review. The results were generally good.

In 1998 the success of our safety and environmental protection efforts was again reflected in awards to individual Roche affiliates. In the United States our plant in Boulder received an award for its pollution prevention efforts from the city's mayor, and the Givaudan Roure plant in East Hanover (New Jersey) was honoured by the New Jersey Water Environment Association for the outstanding quality of its industrial wastewater treatment. The former Boehringer Mannheim plant in Toluca (Mexico) received the Clean Industry Award.

Developments in environmental policy

For many years Roche has been an active contributor to programmes developed by international organisations (including the OECD and CEFIC) that aim to ensure safe management of existing chemicals. Considerable progress has been made, but work is moving forward much more slowly than planned. Accordingly, in 1998 a number of initiatives were launched with the aim of speeding up these programmes and enhancing data gathering on high production volume chemicals. Against this background the chemical and pharmaceutical industries can expect to be faced with increased expenditures for data collection and material assessments in future.

Sustainable development

Roche has long been aware that only companies that are financially successful can be active in the environmental and community spheres—and that environmental and social responsibility are prerequisites for financial success. Roche intends to translate this awareness into action in its daily operations by phasing in innovative, efficient solutions, and thus maintain and strengthen public confidence in the Group wherever it does business.

EXHIBIT 5–9   SPS Technologies, Environmental Disclosures

---

10. Commitments and Contingencies
(thousands of dollars)

Environmental

The Company has been identified as a potentially responsible party by various federal and state authorities for clean-up or removal of waste from various disposal sites. At December 31, 1998, the Company had an accrued liability of $5,500 for environmental remediation, which represents management's best estimate of the undiscounted costs related to environmental remediation that are considered probable and can be reasonably estimated. Management believes the overall costs of environmental remediation will be incurred over an extended period of time. The Company has not included any insurance recovery in the accrued environmental liability. The measurement of the liability is evaluated quarterly based on currently available information. As the scope of the Company's environmental liability becomes more clearly

defined, it is possible that additional reserves may be necessary. Accordingly, it is possible that the Company's results of operations in future quarterly or annual periods could be materially affected. Management does not anticipate that its consolidated financial condition will be materially affected by environmental remediation costs in excess of amounts accrued.

The Company has established procedures for identifying environmental issues at its manufacturing facilities. Environmental and safety coordinators, a designated position at most of the operating facilities, are familiar with environmental laws and regulations and serve as resources for the identification and resolution of environmental issues. The Company also has an environmental audit program, which is used to identify and resolve potential environmental issues at the operating facilities. Through these programs, the Company monitors applicable regulatory developments and manages environmental issues.

In the United States, the Securities and Exchange Commission (SEC) requires disclosure of environmental contingencies and liabilities. This explains why the same KPMG study reports that 70 percent of U.S. companies include financial information on the environment in their annual reports. Regulators and accounting standard setting bodies in a number of countries are in the process of producing requirements for reporting on environmental liabilities and costs. Shareholders and creditors need this information in order to make informed investment and financing decisions.

Exhibit 5–9 on the environment is from the U.S. company SPS Technologies' 1998 annual report, footnotes to the financial statements on commitments and contingencies. In this footnote, SPS discloses to the reader that the company is a potentially responsible party for clean up or removal of waste and has accrued a liability of $5,500,000 for environmental remediation just in case. This required disclosure on the environment has quite a different tone as compared to the voluntary one by Roche.

Although a recent study has shown that U.S. companies provide more environmental information than companies in other areas of the world, the European

Union countries come in second.[3] In fact, each year the European companies that report environmental information have a competition (European Environmental Reporting Awards) to select the best European environmental reporters. The 1998 overall winner of the European awards was the Danish company Novo Nordisk, winning for the third year in a row.

CONCLUSION

Back in the 1960s and 1970s a disclosure explosion took place in most industrially developed countries, mandated by new national laws. Companies began revealing information about themselves that they had never revealed before. A major motivation for such laws seemed to be a low level of investor confidence. Beyond that, companies themselves began to realize that secrecy is self-defeating. Failure to make reasonable disclosures in response to user needs can severely limit the pool of funds available to a corporation. Potential providers of capital, when kept in the dark, will simply put their money elsewhere.

Studies by accountants have shown that firms significantly increase disclosure levels when they seek new sources of investment funds, that differences in disclosure levels among nations are rapidly narrowing, and that increased disclosure can lead to lower costs of capital for business enterprises. These findings are consistent with the arguments made in this and earlier chapters.

Disclosure is a way for the world's multinationals to reach out to shareholders and creditors in other countries without abandoning their own financial accounting practices. Exhibit 4–7 illustrates how the Finnish multinational Valmet accomplishes this. Until the differences in generally accepted accounting principles observed by the world's multinationals can be reconciled and harmonized, disclosure can be a way around the transnational financial reporting problems discussed in Chapter 4.

Most accountants agree that the basic financial statements (balance sheet and income statement) have primacy over disclosures. In other words, such issues as valuing assets and determining net income—the so-called measurement issues—are, for the most part, more important than disclosure issues. Thus, disclosure issues are less controversial, and disclosure requirements tend to be easier to change than accounting measurement rules. Increased disclosure should not be a substitute for improving accounting measurements. Nevertheless, disclosure is an effective way to communicate information that does not fit what is required in financial statements by generally accepted accounting principles. Disclosures need not be constrained by financial reporting rules and are limited only by the imagination of accountants and corporate managements.

---

[3]G. O. Gamble; K. Hsu; C. Jackson; and C. Tollerson. "Environmental Disclosures in Annual Reports: An International Perspective." *The International Journal of Accounting* 31, no. 3 (1996), p. 314.

REVIEW QUESTIONS

1. What is meant by the term *disclosure?* What is the difference between financial and nonfinancial disclosure? What is the difference between required and voluntary disclosure?

2. Why does the worldwide competition for investment funds seem to be propelling increased levels of disclosure by multinational corporations?

3. What is the purpose of presenting financial information by segments?

4. What is the purpose of financial forecast disclosure? Why don't more companies provide them?

5. What kinds of information about shares and shareholders can companies disclose to readers of their financial statements? What is the value of this information to the readers?

6. What is the value added statement? What is the philosophy behind it? Why don't U.S. companies prepare value added statements?

7. Why is there greater emphasis in Europe than in the United States on providing employee and environmental disclosures?

CASES

5–1 and the Winner Is Novo Nordisk!

Last night you attended the European Environmental Reporting Awards ceremony in London. You are the chief financial officer (CFO) of Ford Motor Company and your best friend is the CFO of the United Kingdom company Anglian Water, winner of the recent U.K. environmental reporting award. Anglian Water hopes to come in first place in tonight's competition. Dinner is over and the ceremony begins.

The joint runners-up to first place are Otto Versand of Germany and Anglian Water of the United Kingdom *http://www.anglianwater.co.uk/.* And the winner for the third straight year in a row is Novo Nordisk *http://www.novo.dk/index.asp.*

Questions
1. Why did Novo Nordisk win this prestigious award? (Hint: Go to the Novo Nordisk website to find out.)

2. After browsing through Novo Nordisk's environmental disclosures, you are very impressed. You go to the Ford website (*http://www.ford.com/*) and have a look at what your company reports to the public. What do you see? How do Ford's environmental disclosures compare to Novo Nordisk's? What can Ford do to improve its disclosures?

3. Now find the websites for Anglian Water and Otto Versand. What does each company report? What makes the Novo Nordisk environmental disclosures better?

5–2 Just Another Day at the Exchange

Below are the website addresses for stock exchanges in selected developed countries as well as selected emerging market countries:

London	*www.stockex.co.uk/*
Tokyo	*www.yse.or.jp/*
Prague	*www.pse.cz/*
Mexico	*www.bmv.com.mx/*

Questions

1. Which exchanges are in developed countries? Which exchanges are in emerging market countries?
2. List the disclosure requirements for each exchange for the following items:

   Segment disclosures.

   Financial forecast information.

   Information about shares and shareholders.

   Value added statement.

   Employee disclosures.

   Environmental disclosures.
3. What differences in disclosure requirements do you see across the four exchanges?
4. Which stock exchange makes you feel most comfortable as a prospective investor? Why?

5–3 Corpus Medical Equipment Company

Michael John works in the accounting department of Corpus Medical Equipment Company (CMEC), a U.S. multinational corporation. CMEC manufactures and sells medical equipment used in hospitals and doctors' offices. One of Michael's responsibilities is determining the segment disclosures that CMEC makes in its annual report to shareholders. Since CMEC is in only one product line, Michael's job is basically one of determining how to disclose CMEC's operations by geographic segment.

CMEC sells its products in the following countries, listed alphabetically: Canada, Czech Republic, France, Germany, Hong Kong, Hungary, Italy, Japan, Mexico, Netherlands, Poland, Singapore, Spain, Switzerland, Taiwan, United Kingdom, and United States. Manufacturing facilities are located in three low-wage countries, Mexico, Spain, and Taiwan, plus the United States. The facilities in these countries produce most of the products sold in their respective regions: Asia, Europe, and North America. Over 75 percent of CMEC's revenues are from four countries: Canada, Germany, Japan, and the United States. However, profit margins vary significantly, not only across regions but also across countries within regions. CMEC is just now expanding into Eastern Europe, but is well established in all other markets.

Questions

1. What criteria should Michael consider in determining the geographic segments that should be disclosed in CMEC's annual report?

2. Based on the criteria outlined in question 1, how would you disclose CMEC's operations by geographic segment? In other words, define CMEC's geographic segments. Justify your decision.

ADDITIONAL READINGS

Adams, C. A.; W. Y. Hill; and C. B. Roberts. "Corporate Social Reporting Practices in Western Europe: Legitimating Corporate Behaviour." *British Accounting Review* 30 (1998), pp. 1–21.

Beets, S. D., and C. C. Souther. "Corporate Environmental Reports: The Need for Standards and an Environmental Assurance Service." *Accounting Horizons,* June 1999, pp. 129–45.

Craig, R., and J. Diga. "Corporate Accounting Disclosure in ASEAN." *Journal of International Financial Management & Accounting* 9, no. 3 (1998), pp. 246–74.

Fédération des Experts Comptables Européens. *FEE 1994 Investigation of Emerging Accounting Areas.* London, England: Routledge, 1995. Chapter 4, "Environmental Issues."

Gamble G. O.; K. Hsu; D. Kite; and R. R. Radtke. "Environmental Disclosures in Annual reports and 10Ks: An Examination." *Accounting Horizons,* September 1995, pp. 34–54.

Herrmann, D., and W. B. Thomas. "Geographic Segment Disclosures: Theories, Findings, and Implications." *The International Journal of Accounting* 32, no. 4 (1997), pp. 487–501.

Herrmann, D., and W. Thomas. "Segment Reporting in the European Union: Analyzing the Effects of Country, Size, Industry, and Exchange Listing." *Journal of International Accounting, Auditing & Taxation* 5, no. 1 (1996), pp. 1–20.

Holland, J. *Corporate Communications with Institutional Shareholders: Private Disclosures and Financial Reporting.* Edinburgh: The Institute of Chartered Accountants of Scotland, 1997, 88 pp.

Meek, G. K.; C. B. Roberts; and S. J. Gray. "Factors Influencing Voluntary Annual Report Disclosures by U.S., U.K., and Continental European Multinational Corporations." *Journal of International Business Studies,* Third Quarter 1995, pp. 555–72.

Salter, S. B. "Corporate Financial Disclosure in Emerging Markets: Does Economic Development Matter?" *The International Journal of Accounting* 33, no. 2 (1998), pp. 221–34.

6

MULTINATIONAL CONSOLIDATIONS AND FOREIGN CURRENCY TRANSLATION

LEARNING OBJECTIVES

1. Discuss consolidations from an international perspective, including the reasons why consolidated financial statements are or are not prepared.
2. Know why exchange rates change.
3. Compare the current rate and temporal methods of foreign currency translation.
4. Understand the basic U.S. requirements for foreign currency translation under *FASB Statement No. 52*.
5. Be familiar with foreign currency translation practices in countries outside the United States.

This chapter deals with the preparation of consolidated (group) financial statements by multinational corporations. We first cover consolidation practices around the world and then examine a related issue unique to multinational corporations—foreign currency translation. These topics are complicated and advanced, so our coverage necessarily touches only the basic ideas. Nevertheless, we feel that some knowledge of these topics is important to an initial exposure to international accounting.

THE BASIC IDEA

Consolidated financial statements combine the separate financial statements of two or more companies to yield a single set of financial statements *as if* the individual companies were really one. What is the rationale for preparing consolidated financial statements? Often, a business finds it advantageous to organize itself as a set of separate (legal) corporate entities rather than as one large corporate entity. For example, tax savings sometimes occur because of the way corporate income tax rates are structured. Or a company may separately incorporate the components of its business to limit legal liability. Multinationals are often required by the countries in which they do business to set up a separate corporation in each country. The point is that a *legal* entity is not necessarily the same as an *economic* entity. From an economic point of view, the activities of these various legal entities are centrally administered from corporate headquarters. Thus, the intent of consolidated financial statements is to provide financial accounting information about the group of companies from an overall perspective.

Transactions among the members of a corporate family are not included on consolidated financial statements; only assets, liabilities, revenues, and expenses with external third parties are shown. By law, however, the separate corporate entities are required to keep their own accounting records and to prepare individual financial statements. This means that transactions with other members of the group must be identified so they can be *excluded* when the consolidated statements are prepared. The situation is analogous to preparing combined financial statements for a family. Even though a child may owe a parent some money, from the perspective of the family entity, the liability on the child's personal balance sheet and the receivable on the parent's offset one another. When the child is given his or her weekly allowance, there is a transfer of funds on an individual basis. However, the family unit is no better or worse off as a result. The family's wealth is affected only when that money is given to someone outside the family. Thus, transactions that are all in the family affect individual members but not the family as a whole. The same holds true for corporate "families."

The process of preparing consolidated financial statements involves adding up the individual assets, liabilities, revenues, and expenses reported on the separate financial statements and then *eliminating* the intracompany ones. One company—the *parent*—normally dominates the other *subsidiary* companies. Taking a simple example, assume the following selected items from the individual financial statements of the parent and one subsidiary company:

	Parent	Subsidiary
Cash	$ 100	$ 75
Receivables	360*	280
Payables	90	100*
Revenues	2,000†	2,300
Expenses	1,600	1,900†

*Subsidiary owes Parent $50.

†Subsidiary rented some machinery from Parent for $400.

The $50 receivable that Parent includes on its financial statements and the $50 payable included on Subsidiary's statements represent an intracompany item. Since the purpose of consolidated financial statements is to treat the separate entities as if they were one, it would be incorrect to include this item on the consolidated financial statements. After all, the company cannot owe itself. Similarly, from a consolidated perspective, revenues and expenses would each be overstated by $400 if the rental transaction were included on the consolidated financial statements. Accountants handle these kinds of things by preparing a *consolidated worksheet*, as illustrated by the following:

	Parent	Subsidiary	Eliminations Debit	Eliminations Credit	Consolidated
Cash	$ 100	$ 75			$ 175
Receivables	360	280		50*	590
Payables	90	100	50*		140
Revenues	2,000	2,300	400†		3,900
Expenses	1,600	1,900		400†	3,100

*Intracompany receivable/payable.
† Intracompany revenue/expense.

Thus, on a consolidated basis, receivables are $590; payables are $140; revenues are $3,900; and expenses total $3,100.

To reiterate, the purpose of consolidated financial statements is to present information from an overall perspective about a group of companies under common control and operating as an economic unit.

AN INTERNATIONAL PERSPECTIVE ON CONSOLIDATED FINANCIAL STATEMENTS

Consolidated financial statements first appeared around the turn of the 20th century in the United States. This was a time of great economic expansion during which a number of corporations grew into giants. The era witnessed a wave of corporate mergers. It is said that J. P. Morgan was so proud of his U.S. Steel Company (the first billion-dollar company in the world) that he insisted on preparing and disseminating consolidated financial statements since the company's inception in 1901. Since *holding companies* first became important in the United States, it is not surprising that U.S. accountants were the first to experiment with consolidated financial statements. These statements are now a part of U.S. generally accepted accounting principles.

Holding companies became important in Great Britain and the Netherlands in the 1920s, so consolidated financial statements appeared there somewhat later than in the United States. Today, they are required in both countries. The practice moved much more slowly in the other European countries: German law began requiring consolidations in the 1960s, although for domestic German subsidiaries only. The requirement was extended to all subsidiaries—German and non-German—effective 1990. French law requiring consolidated financial statements was enacted in the late 1980s. In Italy, only companies whose shares are listed on the stock exchange must prepare consolidated statements. In Switzerland large companies and those listed on the stock exchange must prepare them. Japan's requirement dates from 1977.

The observance or nonobservance of consolidated financial statements in a country can be related to several of the variables shaping accounting development discussed in Chapter 1.

1. The Legalistic/Nonlegalistic Orientation of Accounting. Countries with a legalistic approach to accounting tend to focus on the legal entity as the object to be accounted for. In nonlegalistic countries, accounting emphasizes the economic entity. Therefore, consolidated financial statements are less common in legalistic countries, but are the norm in nonlegalistic countries. Nevertheless, the effect of this factor in legalistic countries is becoming less important because of the two factors discussed next.

2. Stock Markets as a Source of External Finance. Group financial statements were first accepted in the United Kingdom and the United States, where stock markets are an important source of external finance. Shareholders rely on the annual report as an important source of information about the company, and they demand a fair presentation of a company's overall financial position and results of operations. Consolidated financial statements are also prepared by multinational corporations—regardless of home country—that have global financing strategies and multiple stock exchange listings. (Thus, the worldwide competition for funds has propelled consolidation practice, a point that is discussed in relation to disclosure issues in Chapter 5.)

3. Political and Economic Ties. Finally, political and economic ties affect this practice. Accounting technology is imported and exported, which is why consolidations are customary in Mexico and the Philippines, countries heavily influenced by the United States. As a result of U.K. influence, such statements are also widespread among British Commonwealth countries such as Australia, Malaysia, and South Africa. A dramatic example occurred within the European Union (EU). The *Seventh Company Law Directive* requiring consolidated accounts was adopted in 1983, and is now in force throughout the EU. Only a few EU countries required consolidated financial statements at the time the *Directive* was adopted. Thus, it had considerable impact in extending consolidation practices within EU member countries. Indeed the effect of EU *Directives* extends to other European countries as well. Some companies from non-EU countries voluntarily comply with EU *Directives* in anticipation of their countries joining the EU.

Preparing consolidated financial statements is now the norm for the world's multinational corporations, and the trend toward consolidated statements is unmistakable. (*Standard 27,* "Consolidated Financial Statements and Accounting for Investments in Subsidiaries," issued by the International Accounting Standards Committee, reinforces this trend. *Standard 27* superceded the earlier *Standard* issued in 1976.) Investors realize that without consolidated financial statements, companies can conceal losses in unconsolidated subsidiaries and thus hide the economic status of the entire group. To illustrate, consider the consolidations example discussed earlier. Suppose that the parent company is operating at below-normal profits. It could increase its own reported profits by increasing the rental charge to the subsidiary above the current amount, shift some of its employees to the subsidiary's payroll, or sell some inventory to the subsidiary at inflated prices. Of course, none of these actions affects group profits, which is why investors prefer consolidated financial statements.

Having argued in favor of consolidated financial statements, we should also point out that they have their limitations. If a company is heavily dependent on a particular product line or on a certain area of the world for its profits, consolidated financial statements can mask such dependencies without additional disclosures. Also, the existence of specific unprofitable operations may be somewhat hidden when blended with the rest of the company. And changing product mixes are harder to detect unless the company provides additional information. For these reasons corporations are increasingly disclosing—on a supplemental basis—detailed accounting information by product line and geographic area. (This subject was explored in Chapter 5.)

FOREIGN CURRENCY TRANSLATION

The foreign subsidiaries of multinational corporations (MNCs) normally keep their accounting records and prepare their financial statements in the currency of the country in which they are located. They do this because it would be too inconvenient to transact business in anything other than the local currency and too impractical to record these transactions in accounting records using another country's currency. As a result, the individual financial statements of a multinational's foreign subsidiaries are expressed in many different currencies. For example, a U.S. multinational corporation may have separate foreign subsidiary financial statements expressed in pounds, pesos, euros, and yen. Yet in order for worldwide consolidated financial statements to be prepared, the subsidiaries' financial statements must all be expressed in a single currency (the U.S. dollar for U.S. multinationals). It is not possible to add up assets, liabilities, revenues, and expenses when they are expressed in different currencies. Therefore, whenever multinational corporations prepare their consolidated financial statements, the financial statements from individual foreign subsidiaries must be *translated* from the currency of the foreign country into the currency of the country where the multinational is headquartered. Foreign currency translation is accomplished using exchange rates.

Exchange Rates

The major currencies of the world are traded in many places and in many ways. An *exchange rate* is the price of one currency relative to another: that is, how much of one currency it takes to buy so much of another currency. Exchange rates are not stable over time; they fluctuate just like the price of nearly everything else does. Exchange rates change for the following reasons:

1. *Trade balance of payments surpluses or deficits.* When a country exports more than it imports, it is said to run a trade balance of payments surplus. Surpluses cause the nation's currency to appreciate in value (i.e., to strengthen). The opposite condition—trade deficits—causes a currency to command less of other nations' currencies.

2. *Relative rates of inflation.* Currencies of countries with higher rates of inflation depreciate relative to the currencies of countries with lower levels of inflation. Generally speaking, inflation means that one is able to buy less and less of everything (including another country's currency) for a fixed amount of one's own currency.

3. *Relative interest rates.* Whenever one nation has higher interest rates relative to other nations, its currency appreciates in value. (Foreigners purchase more of its currency in order to invest in and earn the higher interest.)

4. *Political factors and government intervention.* For international transactions, the currencies of countries considered politically stable tend to be favored over the currencies of unstable countries. Governments also buy and sell currencies when they want to change exchange rates.

Which Exchange Rate(s)?

Given that exchange rates change, a question arises as to which exchange rate should be used to translate the financial statements of a foreign subsidiary. One possibility is the exchange rate at the balance sheet date (i.e., the MNC's fiscal year-end). Accountants often refer to this as the *current,* or *year-end,* exchange rate. However, translating all financial statement items at the rate existing at the balance sheet date is incompatible with historical cost, the basis for current U.S. generally accepted accounting principles.

You can see why in the following example. Suppose a U.S. parent invests $30,000 in a foreign subsidiary and the subsidiary converts the money to its local currency when the exchange rate is 1 LC (local currency) = $1.25. The foreign subsidiary takes its LC 24,000 ($30,000 ÷ 1.25) and buys land. On a historical cost basis, the land has a value of LC 24,000 or $30,000. If by year-end the exchange rate changes to 1 LC = $1.50 and is used to translate the LC 24,000 piece of land, it will appear on the consolidated U.S.-dollar financial statements at $36,000 (LC 24,000 × [1 LC = $1.50]). The piece of land appears to have magically increased in value!

Another possibility is to use the exchange rate when the transaction was first recorded (in this case, when the land was bought, i.e., 1 LC = $1.25). Accountants refer to this as the *historical* exchange rate. This way, the land would always appear on the consolidated balance sheet at $30,000.

Unfortunately, another problem arises when historical exchange rates are used. Since the various assets are acquired at different times, different exchange rates have to be used to translate them. When this happens, the translated balance sheet no longer balances. What to do with the difference between debits and credits is a highly controversial subject among accountants. The amount of the imbalance arises mechanically as a result of the translation process and does not fit the definition of asset, liability, or owners' equity. Yet it has to go somewhere to preserve the accounting equation.

The following example illustrates the point. Assume that on January 1, U.S. Multinational, Inc. (USMI), forms a foreign subsidiary named Foreign Sub. USMI converts $100,000 into Foreign Sub's local currency (LC) at a time when the exchange rate is 1 LC = $1.25. The initial investment, therefore, is LC 80,000. Foreign Sub's opening balance sheet (in local currency and dollars) looks like this:

FOREIGN SUB
Balance Sheet
January 1

Cash	LC 80,000 × (1 LC = $1.25) = $100,000
Owners' equity	LC 80,000 × (1 LC = $1.25) = $100,000

Now, assume that on February 1, when the exchange rate is 1 LC = $1.30, Foreign Sub buys LC40,000 worth of inventory. On February 28, when the exchange rate is 1 LC = $1.40, Foreign Sub buys a fixed asset for LC40,000. The March 1 balance sheet will look like this:

FOREIGN SUB
Balance Sheet
March 1

Inventory	LC 40,000 × (1 LC = $1.30) =	$ 52,000
Fixed asset	LC 40,000 × (1 LC = $1.40) =	$ 56,000
	LC 80,000	$108,000
Owners' equity	LC 80,000 × (1 LC = $1.25) =	$100,000
	LC 80,000	$100,000

While the balance sheet before translation (in local currency) balances, it does not balance after translation into U.S. dollars. In the translated balance sheet, debits exceed credits by $8,000. What to do with the nonexistent credit is a good question, and accountants disagree on the answer.

A conclusion may be apparent to you. Preserving the historical cost basis of accounting by translating foreign financial statements at different historical exchange rates introduces a dangling debit or credit whose nature is difficult to define. That problem can be solved by translating financial statements using a single exchange rate, but the procedure is inconsistent with the historical cost basis of accounting. Either choice involves some undesirable side effects.

Translation Methods Used

U.S. multinational corporations must follow the requirements of *Statement 52*, "Foreign Currency Translation," issued by the Financial Accounting Standards Board (FASB) in 1981. Its provisions will be discussed in a moment. Before *Statement 52*, however, U.S. multinational corporations translated the financial statements of their foreign subsidiaries under the terms of *Statement 8*, issued by the FASB in 1975. *Statement 8* required the use of what is called the *temporal method* of foreign currency translation. Exhibit 6–1 illustrates the temporal method in detail. In general, a mixture of different historical exchange rates and the current exchange rate are used to translate the items on the subsidiary's balance sheet and income statement. The resulting "dangling debit or credit" is treated as a loss or gain on the consolidated income statement. Notice, for example, in Exhibit 6–1 that a $2,500 translation loss is included in the company's consolidated income.

During the years that *Statement 8* was in effect, exchange rates were highly volatile, and because the translation imbalance was required to increase or decrease reported income or loss, corporations experienced more volatility in their reported earnings than managements desired. A volatile earnings pattern normally indicates riskiness, yet managements alleged that translation gains and losses were on paper only—that they had little or no direct effect on actual cash flows. A large number of accountants cried "foul!" and it is fair to say that *Statement 8* was probably the most unpopular Statement ever issued by the FASB. For this reason *Statement 8* was replaced by *Statement 52*.

Under the provisions of *Statement 52*, a foreign subsidiary is classified as either (1) self-sustaining and autonomous or (2) integral to the activities of the parent company. A *self-sustaining, autonomous* subsidiary is one that operates relatively independently from the parent company. Revenues and expenses respond mostly to local conditions, few of the subsidiary's cash flows impact the parent's cash flows, and there are few intracompany transactions with the parent. The local (foreign) currency is said to be its "functional" currency. The balance sheet for a self-sustaining subsidiary is translated at the year-end exchange rate and the income statement at the average-for-the-year exchange rate. There is no effect on reported consolidated earnings from translating the financial statements of autonomous foreign subsidiaries. This so-called *modified current rate method* preserves the balance sheet and income statement financial ratios in U.S. dollars as in the local currency. Exhibit 6–2 illustrates this method.

EXHIBIT 6–1   Illustration of Temporal Method

Assume that the following trial balance, expressed in local currency (LC), is received from a foreign subsidiary. The year-end exchange rate is 1 LC = $1.40, and the average exchange rate for the year is 1 LC = $1.20. Under the temporal method, the trial balance is translated as follows:

1. Inventory and cost of goods sold, at the exchange rate when the inventory was purchased. Assume this is 1 LC = $1.25.

2. Fixed assets and depreciation expense, at the exchange rate when the fixed assets were purchased. Assume this is 1 LC = $0.90.

3. Other balance sheet items, the year-end exchange rate (1 LC = $1.40).

4. Revenues and expenses that are incurred evenly throughout the year (sales and other expenses) at the average exchange rate (1 LC = $1.20).

5. Beginning owners' equity in dollars equals last year's ending owners' equity (translated) in dollars. Assume this is $81,000.

6. A "translation" gain or loss is created to balance the dollar-denominated trial balance.

Thus, the temporal method translation looks like this:

| | Local Currency | | Exchange | U. S. Dollars | |
	Debit	Credit	Rate	Debit	Credit
Cash	LC 15,000		(1 LC = $1.40)	$ 21,000	
Inventory	70,000		(1 LC = $1.25)	87,500	
Fixed assets	35,000		(1 LC = $0.90)	31,500	
Payables		LC 30,000	(1 LC = $1.40)		$ 42,000
Owners' equity					
(beginning)		70,000	—		81,000
Sales		200,000	(1 LC = $1.20)		240,000
Cost of goods sold	120,000		(1 LC = $1.25)	150,000	
Depreciation expense	5,000		(1 LC = $0.90)	4,500	
Other expenses	55,000		(1 LC = $1.20)	66,000	
Translation loss				2,500	
	LC300,000	LC300,000		$363,000	$363,000

On the other hand, an *integral* foreign subsidiary operates as an extension of and is dependent on the parent. Revenues and expenses are largely influenced by the parent, the subsidiary's cash flows directly impact the parent's cash flows, and there are frequent intracompany transactions with the parent. For this type of subsidiary, the U.S. dollar is said to be its "functional" currency. The financial statements of such subsidiaries are translated using the temporal method, illustrated in Exhibit 6–1. (This method has the effect of translating subsidiaries' financial statements as if their transactions originally occurred in U.S. dollars.) In other words, the same temporal method used under *Statement 8* continues to be used under

EXHIBIT 6–2   Illustration of Modified Current Rate Method

Translating the trial balance from Exhibit 6–1 into U.S. dollars would be performed as shown below. (Note that when employing the modified rate method, owners' equity stated in U.S. dollars is a "balancing" amount.)

	Local Currency		Exchange	U. S. Dollars	
	Debit	Credit	Rate	Debit	Credit
Cash	LC 15,000		(1 LC = $1.40)	$ 21,000	
Inventory	70,000		"	98,000	
Fixed assets	35,000		"	49,000	
Payables		LC 30,000	"		$ 42,000
Owners' equity					
(beginning)		70,000	to balance		102,000
Sales		200,000	(1 LC = $1.20)		240,000
Cost of goods sold	120,000		"	144,000	
Depreciation expense	5,000		"	6,000	
Other expenses	55,000		"	66,000	
	LC300,000	LC300,000		$384,000	$384,000

Statement 52 for integral subsidiaries. However, because the financial statements of fewer foreign subsidiaries are now translated using the temporal method, the overall impact of fluctuating exchange rates on reported earnings of U.S. multinational corporations is less.

The Australian, British, and Canadian standards on foreign currency translation basically recommend treatment similar to *Statement 52,* as does *International Accounting Standard 21,* "Accounting for the Effects of Foreign Exchange Rates."

Practice varies in other countries. The EU *Seventh Company Directive* (on consolidations), referred to earlier, does not specify how to translate the financial statements of foreign subsidiaries. Most continental EU countries, including France and Germany, have no standards. Practice is therefore left up to the companies. However, as discussed in Chapter 1, many companies from these countries now follow IASs in preparing their consolidated financial statements. Therefore, they can be expected to comply with *Standard 21.* The Japanese standard requires the current rate method in all circumstances, with translation adjustments shown on the balance sheet as an asset or liability.

The euro was launched in 1999 in 11 of the 15 member countries of the European Union.[1] Conversion is phased in until 2002, when the national currencies of these 11 countries are replaced by a single currency, the euro. The introduction

---

[1] These 11 countries are Austria, Belgium, Finland, France, Germany, Ireland, Italy, Luxembourg, the Netherlands, Portugal, and Spain. Further information about the effects of the euro can be found at *www.euro.fee.be.*

of the euro will simplify foreign currency translation for companies operating in the euro zone. Instead of dealing with up to 11 currencies, now companies need only be concerned with one.

CONCLUSION

Consolidated financial statements are intended to present an overall look at a company's operations and financial position. Unfortunately, for multinational corporations existing accounting tools are not always up on the task. Measuring accounting earnings is an imperfect process anyway, but when fluctuating foreign exchange rates are introduced into that process, it gets even more jumbled. In our opinion, foreign currency translation is one of the most conceptually difficult tasks facing accountants today, and potential solutions do not fit neatly into the traditional accounting framework.

When examining the financial statements of companies from different countries, special care should be taken to understand the companies' consolidation policies and how they translate the financial statements of their foreign operations. The variety of possible methods makes comparing the statements very difficult.

Users of financial statements must also be aware that year-to-year comparisons of profitability are affected by fluctuating exchange rates. For example, a strengthening U.S. dollar buys more of a foreign currency. However, that also means that profits stated in a foreign currency are translated into fewer dollars. Thus, a strengthening dollar dampens a U.S. MNC's consolidated profits. A weaker dollar improves consolidated profits. Untangling the translation effects of fluctuating exchange rates is difficult, if not impossible.

REVIEW QUESTIONS

1. What is the purpose of preparing consolidated financial statements? Why are transactions among the members of a corporate family not included in the consolidated financial statements?

2. How do the following factors influence the practice of preparing consolidated financial statements?

   a. The legalistic/nonlegalistic orientation of accounting.

   b. The stock market as a source of external finance.

   c. Political and economic ties.

3. Why is preparing consolidated financial statements the norm for the world's multinational corporations?

4. What is an exchange rate and why do exchange rates change over time?

5. What does it mean to translate the financial statements of a foreign subsidiary? Why is it necessary to do this before a multinational corporation's consolidated financial statements can be prepared?

6. What does it mean to translate a financial statement item at the historical exchange rate? What does it mean to translate an item at the current exchange rate?

7. Describe the essential features of *FASB Statement 52*, "Foreign Currency Translation."

CASES

6–1 Parent and Subsidiary

The following selected amounts are from the separate financial statements of Parent Company (unconsolidated) and Subsidiary Company:

	Parent	*Subsidiary*
Cash	$ 200	$ 80
Receivables	400	195
Accounts payable	250	110
Retained earnings	790	680
Revenues	4,980	3,520
Rent income	0	215
Dividend income	280	0
Expenses	4,260	2,770

Additional information:

a. Parent owes Subsidiary $80.

b. Parent owns 100 percent of Subsidiary. During the year, Subsidiary paid Parent a dividend of $280.

c. Subsidiary owns the building that Parent rents for $215.

d. During the year, Parent sold some inventory to Subsidiary for $2,200. It had cost Parent $1,400. Subsidiary, in turn, sold the inventory to an unrelated party for $3,000.

Questions

1. What is Parent's (unconsolidated) net income?

2. What is Subsidiary's net income?

3. What is the consolidated profit on the inventory that Parent originally sold to Subsidiary?

4. What are the amounts of the following, on a consolidated basis?

   a. Cash.

   b. Receivables.

   c. Accounts payable.

   d. Revenues.

   e. Expenses.

   f. Dividend income.

   g. Rent income.

   h. Retained earnings.

5. If, instead of consolidated financial statements, Parent presented only its own unconsolidated statements, what kinds of transactions could it engage in with Subsidiary to improve the appearance of its own profitability?

6–2 Beckarove B.V. (A)

Huge Multinational, Inc., received the following trial balance from its overseas subsidiary, Beckarove B.V. It is expressed in Crowns (Cr.).

	Debit	Credit
Cash	4,000	
Inventory	80,000	
Fixed assets (net)	48,000	
Payables		3,000
Capital stock		40,000
Retained earnings (beginning)		60,000
Sales		308,000
Cost of goods sold	228,000	
Salaries	25,000	
Depreciation expense	6,000	
Other expenses	20,000	
	411,000	411,000

Notes: 1. When Beckarove was formed, the exchange rate was 1 Cr. = $0.24. The fixed asset was purchased by Beckarove immediately after formation.

2. At year-end the exchange rate was 1 Cr. = $0.18. The average-for-the-year exchange rate was 1 Cr. = $0.20.

Questions

1. Assume that Beckarove is an autonomous subsidiary. Translate Beckarove's trial balance into U.S. dollars using the modified current rate method required by *FASB Statement 52.*

2. What is Beckarove's net income expressed in Crowns?

3. What is Beckarove's net income expressed in U.S. dollars?

6–3 Beckarove B.V. (B)

Assume the same information as in Beckarove B.V. (A) except that the year-end exchange rate is 1 Cr. = $0.18, and the average-for-the-year exchange rate is 1 Cr. = $0.15.

Questions
1. Translate Beckarove's trial balance into U.S. dollars using the modified current rate method required by *FASB Statement 52.*
2. What is Beckarove's net income expressed in Crowns? How does this compare to the answer you determined in (A)?
3. What is Beckarove's net income expressed in U.S. dollars? How does this compare to the answer you determined in (A)?

6–4 Beckarove B.V. (C)

Refer to the information provided in Beckarove B.V. (A). If Beckarove is deemed an integral subsidiary, Huge Multinational translates Beckarove's trial balance according to the temporal method, as follows:

a. Cash and payables at the year-end exchange rate.

b. Sales, salaries, and other expenses at the average exchange rate.

c. Fixed assets and depreciation expense at the rate in effect when the fixed asset was purchased.

d. Inventory at the rate in effect when purchased. Cost of goods sold at a weighted average rate based on beginning and ending inventory and purchases.

e. Capital stock at the rate in effect when Beckarove was formed.

f. Beginning retained earnings is the translated (U.S.-dollar) balance of the prior year's ending retained earnings.

g. A translation gain (loss) is credited (debited) to bring the dollar-denominated trial balance into balance.

Questions
1. Translate Beckarove's trial balance according to the technique described above. Assume that the relevant exchange rates for inventory and cost of goods sold are 1 Cr. = $0.19 and 1 Cr. = $0.21, respectively. (Other exchange rates are given in Beckarove B.V. (A).) Assume that the translated U.S.-dollar balance of beginning retained earnings is $7,500.
2. What is Beckarove's net income expressed in Crowns?
3. What is Beckarove's net income expressed in U.S. dollars?

ADDITIONAL READINGS

"Accounting for Groups." In J. M. Samuels, R. E. Brayshaw, and J. M. Craner, *Financial Statement Analysis in Europe,* Chapter 7. London: Chapman & Hall, 1995.

Accounting for the Introduction of the Euro. Brussels: European Commission, 1997.

Benjamin, J. J.; S. Grossman; and C. Wiggins. "The Impact of Foreign Currency Translation on Reporting during the Phase-in of SFAS No. 52." *Journal of Accounting, Auditing, and Finance* 1, no. 3 (1996), pp. 174–84.

Cohen, E. "The Euro and Its Impact on the European Economy: A View from Europe." *Journal of International Financial Management & Accounting* 10, no. 2 (Summer 1999), pp. 143–51.

Nobes, C., and R. Parker. "Consolidation." In *Comparative International Accounting,* Chapter 14. Hemel Hempstead: Prentice Hall Europe, 1998.

Fiege, P. "How 'Uniform' Is Financial Reporting in Germany?—The Example of Foreign Currency Translation." *European Accounting Review* 6, no. 1 (1997), pp. 109–22.

Choi, F. D. S.; C. A. Frost; and G. K. Meek. "Foreign Currency Translation." In *International Accounting*, Chapter 6. Upper Saddle River: Prentice Hall, 1999.

Harris, T. S. "Foreign Currency Transactions and Translation." In *International Accounting and Finance Handbook,* Chapter 13. 2nd ed., F. D. S. Choi, ed. New York: John Wiley & Sons, 1997.

Kirsch, R. J., and D. Becker-Dermer. "Proposed Revisions of International Accounting Standard No. 21 and Their Implications for Translation Accounting in Selected English-Speaking Countries." *The International Journal of Accounting* 31, no. 1 (1995), pp. 1–24.

Reither, C. L. "What Are the Best and the Worst Accounting Standards?" *Accounting Horizons* 12, no. 3 (September 1998), pp. 283–92.

7

INTERNATIONAL FINANCIAL STATEMENT ANALYSIS

LEARNING OBJECTIVES

1. Understand how cultural values may influence a country's accounting values.
2. Identify the accounting values that influence a country's accounting system and measurement and disclosure practices.
3. Be aware that when analyzing foreign financial statements, differences exist in timeliness, language, terminology, and format.
4. Be able to access information using the websites provided in the chapter for company research.
5. Recognize that interpreting return, risk, and liquidity ratios requires an understanding of the country's business practices.

Suppose you have just been recently hired as a financial analyst for a major U.S. multinational corporation. Your boss is extremely interested in expanding operations in the Pacific Rim. She has given you a set of financial statements from a Japanese corporation, one with a solid reputation for sustained growth and profitability, which comes highly recommended as an investment opportunity. You sharpen your pencils, get out your calculator, and proceed to apply the ratio analysis techniques you learned as a student. As the company comes so highly recommended, you assume it will be a routine exercise to generate the supporting numbers to back up the purchase decision.

Imagine your surprise when you finish your analysis and discover that the Japanese company is a financial disaster, apparently on the verge of bankruptcy. Its debt-to-equity ratio is nearly twice as large as that of U.S. firms. Contributing to your worries is short-term debt nearly double that of U.S. firms. In addition, the net income numbers are very low compared to what you expected for this growing firm. You are wondering who in the world would recommend this company as an acquisition prospect.

This chapter explores what is wrong with this picture. A *framework* is developed that uses the information from the previous chapters to analyze a foreign-based corporation's financial position in light of the environment in which it operates.

FINANCIAL ACCOUNTING REFLECTS THE ENVIRONMENT IT SERVES

One of the biggest problems in the Japanese scenario described above is the analyst's assumption that U.S. ratio analysis expectations can be "exported" for analyzing foreign financial statements. This is effective only if the foreign financial accounting system and the operating environment closely parallel that of the United States. Chapters 1 through 6 showed that this is rarely the case. Each country's national financial accounting system evolved to serve the needs of its domestic environment and, in particular, the needs of the users of accounting information in that country. Therefore, each country's national financial accounting and reporting requirements are different. The best way to properly analyze financial statements from another country is to understand the domestic accounting system and business practices in that country.

Becoming familiar with each country's accounting and business practices is a monumental task. However, we have the necessary tools. We need to develop an approach—a framework—that we can use with any country.

A FRAMEWORK FOR FINANCIAL STATEMENT ANALYSIS

Environmental Variables

Chapter 1 discussed how an accounting system is shaped by the environment in which it operates. The many variables discussed include external finance, political and economic ties with other countries, the legal system, levels of inflation, the size and complexity of business enterprises, sophistication of management and the financial community, and general levels of education. Exhibit 7–1 compares the U.S. and Japanese environments using these variables. It shows that the two

EXHIBIT 7–1   Environmental Variables

Variable	United States	Japan
External finance	Stock markets	Banks
Political and economic ties with other countries	Influenced by U.K.	Influenced by Germany; later by U.S. after WWII
Legal system	Common law	Code law
Levels of inflation	Low	Low
Size and complexity of business enterprises	Large and complex	Large and complex
Sophistication of management and the financial community	High	High
General levels of education	High	High

countries differ on two critical dimensions, external finance and the legal system. Our analysis begins with an awareness of these differences.

Cultural Values

The accounting system is also influenced by culture and the values that a society shares. Knowing something about a people's values can help us understand their accounting system. Values are defined as a tendency to prefer a certain state of affairs over another. For instance, people in the United States value the concept of individualism, whereas in Japan it is not the individual who is important but how the individual relates to the group. Japanese culture maintains a strong degree of interdependence among individuals, and group norms are far more important than a single individual's opinion or professional judgment.

The Japanese society accepts that there is a natural hierarchical order in which each person has a role that is not questioned. In the United States, we do not accept the notion that power is distributed unequally. In fact, we demand that people have equality.

One final cultural dimension is discussed here—how a society feels about uncertainty and ambiguity. A culture that prefers less uncertainty depends on institutions to maintain conformity, and deviating from the norm or the rule is discouraged, as in Japan. Rules make people comfortable because the rule prescribes what to do in any circumstance, thus removing the uncertainty and need for judgment. The opposite is a society that values practice more than principles and allows for the exception to the rule, as in the United States and the United Kingdom.

Cultural values can be linked to *accounting values,* which gives us some insight into a country's accounting system and its measurement and disclosure practices. Exhibit 7–2 diagrams this link. This concept is explored more fully in the following section.

EXHIBIT 7–2   Culture, Accounting Values, and Accounting Systems—A Framework for Analysis

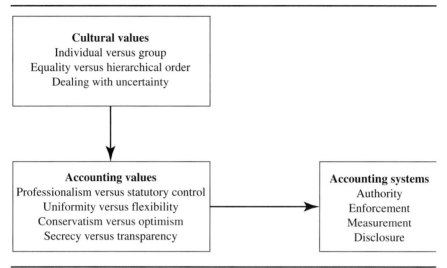

SOURCE: Adapted from S. J. Gray, "Towards a Theory of Cultural Influence on the Development of Accounting Systems Internationally," *Abacus* 24, no. 1 (1988), p. 7. Copyright held by Blackwell Publishers Ltd.

Accounting Values[1]

The following accounting values are not meant to be exhaustive, but are offered as representative of values that influence the development of national accounting systems and measurement and disclosure practices:

Professionalism versus statutory control.

Uniformity versus flexibility.

Conservatism versus optimism.

Secrecy versus transparency.

Knowing something about a country's accounting values helps us to interpret and understand the financial reports of companies operating in that environment. The goal is to be able to realistically analyze the financial reports of any multinational corporation, given the national accounting and business practices that evolved from the operating environment.

Accounting values include a preference for independent *professional judgment* as opposed to *statutory control*. A preference for exercising professional judgment is consistent with a preference for individualism and subjectivity, which we find in the accounting systems of countries listed in the fair presentation/full

---

[1]This section is based on S. J. Gray, "Towards a Theory of Cultural Influence on the Development of Accounting Systems Internationally," *Abacus* 24, no. 1 (1988), pp. 1–15. Copyright held by Blackwell Publishers Ltd.

disclosure model from Chapter 1. The United Kingdom values the concept of presenting a "true and fair view" of a company's financial reports, and the auditor is given the right to use professional judgment to accomplish this goal. Statutory control, or compliance with prescriptive legal requirements, is an accounting value of both the legal compliance and inflation-adjusted models. In Japan, France, and Germany, accountants follow legal rules and exercise much less judgment than in the United Kingdom.

A second set of accounting values that influence financial reporting systems is *uniformity versus flexibility*. A society that values uniformity shows a preference for the enforcement of uniform accounting practices, whereas a society that values flexibility takes into account the circumstances of individual companies. There is a link between this accounting value and the cultural value of dealing with uncertainty that we discussed in the prior section. Uniformity is found in the accounting practices of the code law legal compliance and inflation-adjusted models. Flexibility is exhibited by the countries in the common law fair presentation/full disclosure model. Once again, we see a difference between Japan and the United States; Japan's accounting system is influenced by uniformity, while flexibility prevails in the United States.

The accounting value of *conservatism* relates to the measurement of accounting information and manifests itself in a preference for a cautious approach to measurement as a way to cope with the uncertainty of future events. *Optimism* tolerates more uncertainty in measurement practices. To illustrate, many expenditures made by a company are expected to benefit future periods. Of course, the benefits are uncertain. Should these expenditures be expensed immediately, or should they be shown as an asset and charged to expenses in future periods? Conservatism calls for the former, while optimism would allow the latter in certain situations. The diversity of measurement practices was the topic of Chapter 2. Countries in the fair presentation/full disclosure model take a more optimistic approach to measurement than do those countries of the legal compliance and inflation-adjusted models. The difference in approach has been attributed to different providers of capital and the demands of different users as well as the influence of tax laws. For example, Japanese financial accounting is strongly influenced by the tax law, which leads to more conservative measurement practices in order to minimize taxes.

The last set of accounting values we discuss here is *secrecy* versus *transparency* in regard to disclosure practices, which was the topic of Chapter 5. The countries of the legal compliance and inflation-adjusted models show a preference for confidentiality and tend to restrict disclosure of information to management and those who provide the business financing. Secrecy and conservatism are related in that both result in a more cautious approach to reporting, as is seen in Japan. The fair presentation/full disclosure model countries disclose more information and take a more publicly accountable approach to financial reporting, which is their response to the providers of capital being private investors. Exhibit 7–3 offers a matching of accounting values with the three accounting models discussed in Chapter 1.

EXHIBIT 7–3   Accounting Models and Accounting Values

Fair Presentation/Full Disclosure	*Legal Compliance*	*Inflation-Adjusted*
Professionalism	Statutory control	Statutory control
Flexibility	Uniformity	Uniformity
Optimism	Conservatism	Conservatism
Transparency	Secrecy	Secrecy

ANALYSIS OF FINANCIAL INFORMATION

Timeliness, Language, Terminology, and Format

In the United States, corporate annual reports are published in a timely fashion, which adds relevance to the information's usefulness. In fact, this is more or less taken for granted. Companies must file their financial statements with the Securities and Exchange Commission within 90 days after their year-end. However, users may experience delays in the receipt of foreign financial information. Exhibit 7–4 provides insight into the number of days that elapse between a company's fiscal year-end and the date of the auditor's report. (The date of the auditor's report normally corresponds to the date the annual report is made public.) Notice that an average of more than 90 days elapsed between the fiscal year-end and the date of the auditor's report for the companies observed from France, Germany, and Hong Kong. Companies from the United States, Brazil, South Korea, and Mexico averaged less than 60 days. Generally financial information is publicly available sooner in the United States.

For English-speaking users, a barrier to usefulness exists if the report is not in English. Companies will naturally publish their reports in the national language of their country and then consider translating to second and perhaps third languages. Chapter 4 discussed convenience translations. Most large companies in developed economies of non-English speaking countries provide English language translations of all or part of their annual reports. It appears that English is becoming the accepted language of business and that the language barrier is no longer an insurmountable problem.

Differences in accounting terminology also present a communication problem. Several terms in a U.K. annual report could confuse the American user. Stocks refer to inventory, receivables are called debtors, and payables are called creditors. Fixed assets refer to all assets retained for continuous use, not just property, plant, and equipment. The profit and loss account refers to the income statement and turnover means sales. Reserves usually refers to retained earnings.

The format of the British balance sheet is the opposite of a U.S. balance sheet with assets and liabilities running from lowest to highest liquidity. Fixed assets appear above current assets. The user of foreign financial statements must be

---

EXHIBIT 7–4   Average Delay between Year-End Date and Date of Auditor's Report

---

Number of Days	Countries
1–30	None
31–60	Brazil
	Canada
	Mexico
	South Korea
	Taiwan
	United States
61–90	Argentina
	Australia
	Denmark
	Japan
	Netherlands
	Singapore
	Spain
	United Kingdom
91–120	France
	Germany
	Hong Kong
121 and over	Pakistan

SOURCE: This table was prepared using data presented in *International Accounting and Auditing Trends,* 4th ed., ed., Vinod B. Bavishi and Center for International Financial Analysis & Research, Inc. (Princeton: CIFAR Publications, Inc., 1995), vol. II.

observant and a little suspicious because things that appear familiar may in fact be quite different.

Convenience translations were discussed in Chapter 4. In this case, the user must be careful to notice that both the language and the monetary amounts have been translated for the user; however, the statements are still in foreign generally accepted accounting principles (GAAP) and cannot be directly compared to those of the user's home country. Chapter 4 also discussed the fact that some multinationals provide limited restatements or secondary financial statements based on another set of GAAP, such as that of the International Accounting Standards Committee. Even if readers get financial statements in a language, currency unit, and based on accounting principles that they understand, they must still consider one additional point. Financial practices (as opposed to accounting practices) and business decision making differ around the world, and readers of foreign financial statements must understand how the business environment in a corporation's home country affect the firm's financial reports. This is especially critical if the user is comparing the accounting numbers of companies from different cultures. One device used to analyze financial reports is ratio analysis, which is discussed in a later section.

EXHIBIT 7–5 Websites for Company Research

- CAROL (Company Annual Reports On Line), a free service offering online access to European Company Annual Reports (*http://www.carol.co.uk*).
- The U.S. Securities and Exchange Commission's Edgar website (*http://www.sec.gov/edgarhp.htm*) provides free access to annual reports on Form 10-K filed with the Commission by public domestic companies.
- Many stock exchange websites provide links to listed company websites. For example, see *http://www.nyse.com* (New York Stock Exchange), *http://www.nasdaq.com* (Nasdaq), *http://www.amex.com* (American Stock Exchange), *http://www.bourse-de-paris.fr* (Paris Bourse), and *http://www.aex.nl* (Amsterdam Exchanges).
- For ratings and reviews of hundreds of business-oriented websites: *http://businessdirectory.dowjones.com*.
- For free information such as press releases, links to company home pages and other information, including more than 800 of the most important non-U.S. companies: *http://www.hoovers.com*.

SOURCE: F. D. S. Choi, C. A. Frost, and G. K. Meek, *International Accounting* (Englewood Cliffs, N.J.: Prentice Hall, 1999), p. 313.

Access to Information

Suppose you wanted to review the annual report of Suzuki Motor Corporation. You could write to this Japanese company and request that they send you a copy. You could call the company directly and try to communicate with the person who answers the phone. Or you could access information directly and quickly from the Suzuki website (*http://www.suzuki.co.jp/*). Exhibit 7–5 provides a list of useful websites for researching companies.

Ratio Analysis

Ratios of key items on the financial statements are calculated to determine such things as rate of return, riskiness, and the ability to pay debts (liquidity).

Indicators of Return.   Two popular ratios that provide the investor with information as to the rates of return on a particular investment are earnings per share and return on investment. Earnings per share gives the investor an indication of the earnings attributable to each share of stock and is calculated as follows:

$$\text{Earnings per share} = \frac{\text{Net income accruing to common stock}}{\text{Total shares of common stock outstanding}}$$

Return on investment indicates how efficiently capital has been employed by the company. Investment may be defined as total assets or as owners' equity. The asset base is used to indicate the return that the company generates on its asset commitment. Investors use return on equity when they are interested in the return that accrues to them on their contributed capital as common shareholders. The ratios are calculated as follows:

$$\text{Return on assets} = \frac{\text{Net income}}{\text{Total assets}}$$

$$\text{Return on equity} = \frac{\text{Net income}}{\text{Owners' equity}}$$

Indicators of Liquidity and Risk.   The ratios used to indicate liquidity and risk are the current ratio and the debt-to-equity ratio. The current ratio indicates the company's ability to pay its short-term creditors with its most liquid assets, the current assets. It is calculated as follows:

$$\text{Current ratio} = \frac{\text{Current assets}}{\text{Current liabilities}}$$

The debt-to-equity ratio provides the investor with another indicator of the relative risk of this investment. As the name implies, this ratio relates debt (investment provided by creditors) to equity (investment provided by owners). The more you rely on debt versus equity to finance your business, the more risk you face. Therefore, the higher the debt-to-equity ratio, the less safe is your business. Generally speaking, creditors should be more willing to lend money to, and investors should be more willing to invest money in, companies with lower debt-to-equity ratios. The reader should note that this is a very U.S. interpretation of the debt-to-equity ratio. More is said about this later. This ratio is computed as follows:

$$\text{Debt-to-equity} = \frac{\text{Total liabilities}}{\text{Owners' equity}}$$

Suzuki Motor Corporation

We use the consolidated five-year summary of financial statements of Suzuki (Exhibit 7–6) to practice our financial statement analysis skills in the Japanese environment. Footnote #1 to the financial statements (Exhibit 7–7) alerts us to the fact that the statements have been translated to English and to U.S. dollars, but the GAAP remain Japanese. Our first step is to calculate the ratios, and then we interpret them. (While the ratios are calculated in U.S. dollars below, they would be the same in Japanese yen.) Earnings per share is taken directly from Exhibit 7–6, Suzuki's consolidated five-year summary, and is reported to be $0.508.

$$\text{Return on assets} = \frac{\$228,287}{\$7,852,239} = 2.91\%$$

$$\text{Return on equity} = \frac{\$228,287}{\$2,835,477} = 8.05\%$$

$$\text{Current ratio} = \frac{\$4,400,670}{\$4,347,599} = 1.01$$

EXHIBIT 7–6   Consolidated Five-Year Summary, Suzuki Motor Corporation
Thousands of U.S. dollars (Note B) (except per share amounts)

Years ended 31st March	1998	1997	1996	1995	1994
Net sales	$11,270,139	$11,373,390	$10,455,205	$9,525,249	$9,288,132
Net income	228,287	254,249	201,565	151,833	115,392
Net income per share:					
Primary	0.508	0.566	0.449	0.338	0.260
Fully diluted	0.504	0.562	0.445	—	—
Cash dividends per share	0.056	0.064	0.064	0.056	0.056
Shareholders' equity	2,835,477	2,636,740	2,409,856	2,242,667	2,119,707
Total current assets	4,400,670	4,569,123	4,369,566	3,956,887	3,379,875
Total assets	7,852,239	7,642,934	7,211,226	6,630,300	6,038,716
Depreciation and amortization	509,183	455,911	432,816	488,817	470,197

Note B: Yen amounts have been translated into U.S. dollars, for convenience only, at ¥132.10 = US$1, the prevailing exchange rate on 31 March 1998.

EXHIBIT 7–7   Notes to Consolidated Financial Statements

1. Basis of presenting consolidated financial statements
   The accompanying consolidated financial statements of SUZUKI MOTOR CORPORA-TION (the Company) have been prepared on the basis of generally accepted accounting principles and practices in Japan, and from the consolidated financial statements filed with the Minister of Finance as required by the Securities and Exchange Law of Japan.
   Certain reclassifications and modifications have been made to the original consolidated financial statements for the convenience of readers outside Japan. In addition, the consolidated statements of shareholders' equity have been prepared as additional information, although such statements are not required in Japan, and the notes include information that is not required under generally accepted accounting principles and practices in Japan.
   All yen figures have been rounded down to millions of yen. For the convenience of readers, the consolidated financial statements have been presented in U.S. dollars by translating all Japanese yen amounts on the basis of ¥132.10 to U.S.$1, the rate of exchange prevailing as of 31 March, 1998. Consequently, the totals shown in the consolidated financial statements (both in yen and in U.S. dollars) do not necessarily agree with the sum of the individual amounts.

Total current liabilities are reported on the consolidated balance sheet of Suzuki, which is not reproduced here. Total debt is calculated by subtracting shareholders' equity from total assets ($7,852,239 − $2,835,477 = $5,016,762) as given on the consolidated five-year summary.

$$\text{Debt-to-equity} = \frac{\$5,016,762}{\$2,835,477} = 1.77$$

Exhibit 7–8 compares sales, net income, and leverage figures across companies from Japan and the United States. Average sales figures are higher for Japanese companies because Japanese firms traditionally seek maximum sales and market share. Average net income numbers are much higher for U.S. companies due to a less conservative (more optimistic) approach to reporting net income. (Remember that conservatism is an accounting value exhibited by countries, like Japan, that fall into the legal compliance model.) Japanese firms rely on bank financing and generally carry more debt than U.S. firms as part of their capital structure. Therefore, Japanese firms have higher average debt-to-equity ratios than U.S. firms do.

Exhibit 7–9 provides additional evidence that Japanese firms underreport earnings compared to U.S. firms. This underreporting of earnings results in the price-earnings ratios for Japanese firms being higher than U.S. firms. In general, indicators of return and profitability for Japanese companies are often lower, as they are for Suzuki, than for U.S. companies because there is less pressure in Japan to report steadily increasing net income. This underreporting of earnings is partially caused by differences in Japanese and U.S. GAAP. But there is more to this difference than just GAAP. This difference is also driven by differences in business practices. Remember that Japan fits in the legal compliance accounting model and the United States fits in the fair presentation/full disclosure model. Therefore, we must take these differences into consideration as we interpret the ratios we calculated for Suzuki.

Suzuki exhibits typical financial characteristics of a Japanese company. The current ratio is low, indicating that there is quite a bit of current debt relative to current assets. (Most industry averages for the current ratio of U.S. firms range between 1.50 and 1.90.) Japanese investors would not find this ratio troubling because in Japan short-term borrowing is preferred to long-term debt. (Suzuki's long-term debt is only $606,341.) This allows for more frequent adjustment of interest rates on the debt and lowers interest expense, as short-term rates are usually lower than long-term. The short-term debt is continuously renewed and so serves the purpose of long-term debt and substitutes for longer-term borrowing. In addition, it is not unusual for Japanese companies to carry substantial amounts of accounts payable, as terms of payment are extremely favorable. This type of trade credit serves as a form of longer-term financing provided by major suppliers to their friends.

The debt-to-equity ratio is somewhat high at 1.77. (U.S. firms average 1.50.) Suzuki's debt makes up 64 percent of total liabilities and stockholders' equity, which is high, compared to the typical U.S. firm. Equity financing is not as available in Japan as it is the United States, and it is more expensive than debt financing. Therefore, banks have historically been the main providers of capital.

Putting It All Together

Our analysis shows us that significant differences exist between the United States and Japanese economic environments, cultural values, and accounting

EXHIBIT 7–8   Financial Characteristics of Japanese and U.S. Firms[a]

	Japan	United States
Average sales ($U.S. millions)	2,053.024	1,645.580
Average net income ($U.S. millions)	−15.522	50.413
Average leverage (debt/equity)	2.032	0.514

[a]This table presents summary statistics for 160 sample firms, 80 each domiciled in Japan and the United States, matched on market value of equity (as of late calendar 1993) and all drawn from the manufacturing industry group (SIC codes 20-39).

SOURCE: F. D. S. Choi, C. A. Frost, and G. K. Meek, *International Accounting* (Englewood Cliffs, N.J.: Prerntice Hall, 1999), p. 301.

EXHIBIT 7–9   Average Price-Earnings Ratio Data of Companies Listed on the Tokyo Stock Exchange and the New York Stock Exchange

	Tokyo Stock Exchange[*]	New York Stock Exchange[■]
1988	58.4	14.2
1989	70.6	13.8
1990	39.8	14.7
1991	37.8	20.1
1992	36.7	25.4
1993	64.9	23.3
1994	74.5	15.1
1995	86.5	19.1
1996	79.3	15.7
1997	37.6	17.4

[*]Tokyo Stock Exchange, *Fact Book,* 1998
[■]New York Stock Exchange Fact Book—1998.

`SOURCE: M. E. Haskins, K. R. Ferris, and T. I. Selling, *International Financial Reporting and Analysis* (Burr Ridge, IL.: Richard D. Irwin, 2000), p.350.

values. As financial analysts we cannot simply compare U.S. and Japanese company financial statements. From Chapter 2 we know that a great deal of diversity in generally accepted accounting principles exists between the United States and Japan. We know that Japanese business practices are influenced by the cultural values embraced by the Japanese people. We must study the Japanese business environment in order to interpret the financial information that we see on Suzuki's financial statements. We know that the differences we see in return (profitability), riskiness, and liquidity ratios are the result of the way the Japanese conduct their business affairs (e.g., reporting lower net income for tax purposes, long-term focus on the "bottom line," and use of short-term debt for financing assets), and are not necessarily indicators of financial weakness.

CONCLUSION

This chapter develops a *framework* for international financial statement analysis that can be used to analyze the financial reports of foreign multinational corporations. Once again, the analysis begins with a review of the environmental variables that shape a country's accounting system. Then the analysis includes attention to culture and the specific societal values that influence accounting values and, ultimately, accounting systems and measurement and disclosure practices. Analysts must pay attention to the timeliness, language, terminology, and format of foreign financial reports. In addition, they must always be aware of the fact that the foreign statements generally represent foreign GAAP. When analysts interpret the financial ratios, they must keep in mind that business practices are culturally based and can have a significant impact on a company's financial statements.

REVIEW QUESTIONS

1. Exhibit 7–1 compares the U.S. and Japanese environments along several environmental variables. Add a column for Germany and then compare all three countries. (Hint: You might try looking on the Web for environmental information on any country that you are analyzing.)

2. How do the cultural values discussed in the chapter affect the accountant's role as a provider of useful information?

3. How do the accounting values of statutory control and uniformity influence the accountant's role as a provider of useful information?

4. How do the accounting values of conservatism and secrecy affect information that you expect to find in the annual reports of foreign corporations?

5. As a prospective investor, you write to Toyota, a Japanese automaker, and ask for a copy of its most recent annual report. You receive a beautiful and thorough report in English and in U.S. dollars. You are delighted that Toyota makes its report so investor friendly. Why must you be careful as you proceed with your analysis?

6. As a prospective investor, you write to British Airways of the United Kingdom for a copy of its most recent annual report. In what ways would you expect the financial statements to be similar to those of United Airlines? What differences would you expect to find?

7. Return to the financial information of Suzuki in Exhibit 7–6. As a prospective investor, which items on the financial statements would you like to explore more fully? Why?

CASES

7–1 British Telecommunications (BT)

British Telecommunications is incorporated in the United Kingdom and is in the process of transforming itself from a U.K. telecommunications company into a global communications company. We will use the consolidated profit and loss account and the consolidated balance sheet of BT to help us, as prospective investors, analyze, interpret, and understand BT's financial results.

Questions

1. Comment on the differences in terminology and format between British- and American-style balance sheets and income statements.

2. Prepare a balance sheet for BT that follows the American-style format.

3. Select some financial ratios that are of interest to you in your analysis. Why have you selected these particular ratios? What do the results of your ratio analysis tell you about the financial health of BT?

4. What will you need to do if you want to compare your results for BT to those of AT&T?

Group profit and loss account

For the year ended 31 March 1999	Notes	*Before exceptional items* *1999* *£m*	*Exceptional items* *1999* *£m*	*After exceptional items* *1999* *£m*	*1998* *£m*	*1997* *£m*
Total turnover —ongoing activities	2	**18,223**		**18,223**	16,039	15,021
—discontinued activities	2	—	—	—	1,372	2,358
Total turnover, including discontinued activities	2	**18,223**	—	**18,223**	17,411	17,379
Group's share of joint ventures' turnover	2	**(561)**	—	**(561)**	(147)	(80)
Group's share of associates' turnover	2	**(709)**	—	**(709)**	(1,624)	(2,364)

(Continued) For the year ended 31 March 1999	Notes	**Before exceptional items 1999 £m**	**Exceptional items 1999 £m**	**After exceptional items 1999 £m**	*1998 £m*	*1997 £m*
Group turnover —ongoing activities	2	**16,953**	**—**	**16,953**	15,640	14,935
Other operating income (*a*)	3	**168**	**—**	**168**	372	106
Operating costs	4	**(13,236)**	**(69)**	**(13,305)**	(12,355)	(11,796)
Group operating profit— ongoing activities		**3,885**	**(69)**	**3,816**	3,657	3,245
Group's share of operating loss of joint ventures	5	**(342)**	**—**	**(342)**	(199)	(36)
Group's share of operating profit (loss) of associates	5	**—**	**—**	**—**	3	220
Total operating profit:						
Ongoing activities		**3,543**	**(69)**	**3,474**	3,436	3,209
Discontinued activities		**—**	**—**	**—**	25	220
		3,543	**(69)**	**3,474**	3,461	3,429
Profit on sale of fixed asset investments	6	**—**	**1,107**	**1,107**	—	—
Profit on sale of group undertakings	6	**—**	**—**	**—**	63	8
Interest receivable	7	**165**	**—**	**165**	162	209
Interest payable	8	**(451)**	**—**	**(451)**	(472)	(383)
Premium on repurchase of bonds	9	**—**	**—**	**—**	—	(60)
Profit on ordinary activities before taxation		**3,257**	**1,038**	**4,295**	3,214	3,203

(concluded) For the year ended 31 March 1999	Notes	Before exceptional items 1999 £m	Exceptional items 1999 £m	After exceptional items 1999 £m	1998 £m	1997 £m
Tax on profit on ordinary activities:						
Corporation and similar taxes	10	**(1002)**	**(291)**	**(1,293)**	(977)	(1,102)
Windfall tax	10	**—**	**—**	**—**	(510)	—
		(1,002)	**(291)**	**(1,293)**	(1,487)	(1,102)
Profit on ordinary activities after taxation		**2,255**	**747**	**3,002**	1,727	2,101
Minority interests	11	**(19)**	**—**	**(19)**	(25)	(24)
Profit for the financial year		**2,236**	**747**	**2,983**	1,702	2,077
Dividends:						
Ordinary	12			**(1,322)**	(1,216)	(1,266)
Special	12			**—**	—	(2,244)
				(1,322)	(1,216)	(3,510)
Retained profit (transfer from reserves) for the financial year	26			**1,661**	486	(1,433)
Basic earnings per share	13			**46.3p**	26.6p	32.8p
Basic earnings per share before exceptional items	13			**34.7p**	31.7p	32.8p
Diluted earnings per share	13			**45.3p**	26.2p	32.2p
Diluted earnings per share before exceptional items	13			**34.0p**	31.2p	32.2p
(a) Including MCI break up fee net of expenses				**—**	238	—

Balance sheets

		Group		Company	
		1999	*1998*	*1999*	*1998*
At 31 March 1999	*Notes*	*£m*	*£m*	*£m*	*£m*
Fixed assets					
Intangible assets	17	**742**	—	**—**	—
Tangible assets	18	**17,854**	17,252	**15,022**	14,899
Investments in joint ventures:	19				
Share of gross assets and goodwill		**1,857**	524		
Share of gross liabilities		**(775)**	(274)		
		1,082	250		
Investments in associates	19	**418**	143		
Other investments	19	**332**	1,315		
Total investments	19	**1,832**	1,708	**12,371**	7,808
Total fixed assets		**20,428**	18,960	**27,393**	22,707
Current assets					
Stocks		**159**	145	**134**	124
Debtors	20	**3,995**	3,387	**5,976**	4,918
Investments	21	**3,278**	731	**1,897**	15
Cash at bank and in hand		**102**	62	**7**	1
Total current assets		**7,534**	4,325	**8,014**	5,058
Creditors: amounts falling due within one year					
Loans and other borrowings	22	**947**	881	**7,250**	3,282
Other creditors	23	**7,082**	6,081	**7,008**	6,043
Total creditors: amounts falling due within one year		**8,029**	6,962	**14,258**	9,325
Net current liabilities		**(495)**	(2,637)	**(6,244)**	(4,267)
Total assets less current liabilities		**19,933**	16,323	**21,149**	18,440
Creditors: amounts falling due after more than one year					
Loans and other borrowings	22	**3,386**	3,889	**4,289**	4,126
Provisions for liabilities and charges	24	**1,391**	1,426	**1,116**	1,269
Minority interests		**216**	223	**—**	—
Capital and reserves					
Called up share capital	25	**1,617**	1,603	**1,617**	1,603
Share premium accounting	26	**1,206**	892	**1,206**	892
Other reserves	26	**774**	776	**747**	749
Profit and loss accounting	26	**11,343**	7,514	**12,174**	9,801
Total equity shareholders' funds	26	**14,940**	10,785	**15,744**	13,045
		19,933	16,323	**21,149**	18,440

Debtors include amounts receivable after more than one year: group £nil (1998—£97m) and company £nil (1998—£213m).

The financial statements on pages 59 to 103 were approved by the board of directors on 25 May 1999 and were signed on its behalf by

Sir lain Vallance *Chairman*

Sir Peter Bonfield CBE *Chief Executive*

R P Brace *Group Finance Director*

7–2 BT or Suzuki?

You have some extra money to invest in the stock market and are trying to decide between buying stock in BT or Suzuki. You just recently visited the United Kingdom and some of its pubs and feel like you are beginning to understand the British. Next year you plan to go on an exchange program to Japan and you have always admired the way the Japanese conduct business.

Questions
1. Outline the steps that you would follow to compare the financial results of BT to Suzuki.
2. How will you analyze the operating environment of each company?
3. Compare the rates of return, riskiness, and liquidity of the two companies.
4. Which company will you invest in? You must choose one or the other.

7–3 Croissant avec Café au Lait

So far, much of our attention has been focused on the United States, Japan, the United Kingdom, and Germany. Let's add France to the list of countries that we are learning more about. France is the home of Paris and the Eiffel Tower, the Louvre and Monet, Euro Disney and the Bourse de Paris, and Peugeot, L'Oreal, and Pernod Ricard.

Questions
1. Exhibit 7–5 provides a list of websites for company research. Using CAROL, identify a French multinational company that you would like to know more about.
2. Now, use the NYSE website (also found in Exhibit 7–5) to see if the company you have identified is listed on the NYSE.
3. Complete Exhibits 7–1 and 7–3 for France.
4. Analyze the financial statements of the multinational you identified using the same step-by-step framework that we used for Suzuki.
5. Comment on the differences in timeliness, terminology, format, and disclosure between French- and American-style financial statements. Does the French company provide a statement of cash flow?
6. Interpret the results of your analysis given what you have learned about the French business environment, the cultural variables influencing business practices and financial reporting, and the French accounting system.

ADDITIONAL READINGS

Bindon, K. R., and H. Gernon. "The European Union: Regulation Moves Financial Reporting Toward Comparability." *Research in Accounting Regulation* 9 (1995), pp. 23–48.

Capstaff, J.; K. Paudyal; and W. Rees. "Analysts' Forecasts of German Firms' Earnings: A Comparative Analysis." *Journal of International Financial Management & Accounting* 9, no. 2 (1998), pp. 83–116.

Das, S., and S. Saudagaran. "Accuracy, Bias, and Dispersion in Analysts' Earnings Forecasts: The Case of Cross-Listed Foreign Firms." *Journal of International Financial Management & Accounting* 9, no. 1 (1998), pp. 16–33.

Godwin, J. H.; S. R. Goldberg; and E. B. Douthett. "Relevance of U.S. GAAP for Japanese Companies." *The International Journal of Accounting* 33, no. 5 (1998), pp. 587–604.

Kim, E. Y. *A Cross-Cultural Reference of Business Practices in a New Korea.* Westport, Connecticut: Quorem Books, 1996, 179 pp.

King, R. D., and J. C. Langli. "Accounting Diversity and Firm Valuation." *International Journal of Accounting* 33, no. 5 (1998), pp. 529–67.

Meek, G. K., and C. L. Fulkerson. "Analysts' Earnings Forecasts and the Value Relevance of 20-F Reconciliations from non-U.S. to U.S. GAAP." *Journal of International Financial Management & Accounting* 9, no. 1 (1998), pp. 1–15.

Morriss, M. W.; K. Y. Williams; K. Leung; R. Larrick; M. T. Mendoza; D. Bhatnagar; J. Li; M. Kondo; J. L. Luo; and J. C. Hu. "Conflict Management Style: Accounting for Cross-National Differences." *Journal of International Business Studies* 29, no. 4 (1998), pp. 729–48.

Ralston, D. A.; C. P. Egri; S. Stewart; R. H. Terpstra; and Y. Kaicheng. "Doing Business in the 21st Century with the New Generation of Chinese Managers: A Study of Generational Shifts in Work Values in China." *Journal of International Business Studies* 30, no. 2 (1999), pp. 415–28.

Zarzeski, M. T. "Spontaneous Harmonization Effects of Culture and Market Forces on Accounting Disclosure Practices." *Accounting Horizons* (March 1996), pp. 18–37.

8

INFORMATION SYSTEMS FOR MULTINATIONAL PLANNING AND CONTROL

LEARNING OBJECTIVES

1. Gain familiarity with the nature of business information systems and the functions they perform.
2. Be able to explain the different forms of organization used by multinational corporations (MNCs) to coordinate worldwide activities.
3. Understand how top managements of MNCs determine policies for operating in the international environment.
4. Identify communication problems that challenge the effectiveness of the MNC planning and control system.
5. Recognize the complexity of planning for the transnational corporations of the next century.

We live in the Information Age. The integration of the telephone, the computer, and television is producing the "information highway." Information feeds managerial decision making and control. In international business operations, the information system provides the information that the multinational corporation (MNC) needs to plan, control, evaluate, and coordinate all of its business activities.

It is senior management's responsibility to maximize the economic well-being of the MNC as an international entity, which normally translates to maximizing long-run profits globally.

This is not as easy as it sounds. The profit strategies of Japanese managers are more long-run than those of U.S. managers. Germans often base profit goals on costs incurred, the Swiss are more oriented to "what the market will bear," and Italians usually like to negotiate. Scandinavian countries control MNCs based there rather tightly, whereas Holland does not. Thus, accounting information needs vary not only from country to country and culture to culture, but also between central management (headquarters) and individual country managements.

Earlier chapters dealt with reporting information to users *external* to the MNC (stockholders, creditors, employees, and customers). Much of the information reported externally is required in the form of annual reports. Our attention now turns to the information needs of *internal* users—MNC management.

Management uses internal information to plan, control, and evaluate in both the short and long run. For example, short-run budgets are determined for the operating year and then used to determine how well managers have run their business unit, say, a subsidiary company located in another country. Long-run budgets may be developed for five years—thus the short-range annual budgeting process is turned into a long-range strategic plan for the MNC and all of its subsidiaries.

Managers at all levels in the MNC need internally developed and reported information to monitor and improve their decision making. An MNC's information system must incorporate and report changes in the economic and political environments, legal constraints, cultural differences and fads, and sociological differences in each country of operation. This information is generally provided by the subsidiary managers and includes notice of anticipated changes in the exchange rates, in political ideology (e.g. the downfall of Communism), or even in teenage buying habits (from heavy-metal rock groups to rappers). Such external conditions are considered when designing an information system for a single-country situation, so imagine how important this information is to the MNC that operates in multiple countries. The quality and quantity of information received by management is critical to achieving the goals of the entire multinational organization. Exhibit 8–1 can be used to visualize the pervasiveness of the impact of environmental variables on an MNC's information and control systems.

MNC ORGANIZATION AFFECTS THE INFORMATION SYSTEM

An MNC has various levels of managers with varying degrees of authority and responsibility. The distribution of these management levels constitutes the MNC *organizational structure* and determines what information each level needs to plan and control its operations. The information needs define how the data are collected and processed within the information system. Therefore, the structure of

EXHIBIT 8–1   Framework for Multinational Financial Control

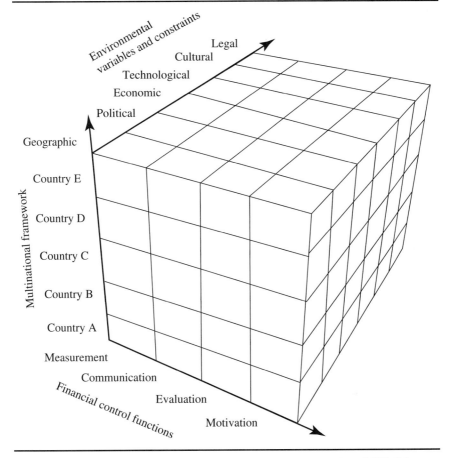

SOURCE: Frederick D. S. Choi and Gerhard G. Mueller, *International Accounting* (Englewood Cliffs, N.J.: Prentice Hall, 1992), p. 475.

data collecting, processing, and reporting within an information system ought to parallel and complement the organizational structure of the MNC.

Transnational Organizational Capability

Companies seeking success in the competitive world of the 21st century must be simultaneously local and global. This crossover of business emphasis has triggered much definitional confusion. The media and professional journals not only refer to companies as international, multinational, transnational, and global, but they add modifiers like multicultural, nonhierarchical, globally integrated, and borderless.

For our purposes, we use the term MNC (multinational corporation) throughout this book in a broad generic sense to cover *all* companies whose activities regularly cross national boundaries. At the same time we recognize, especially in the context of this chapter on systems and control, that MNC organizational structures are different from company to company, are constantly undergoing change, and have "flattened out" in response to information technology advances.[1]

As we explore MNC organizational aspects further, the reader should keep in mind that the classic *multinational* company has operated as a decentralized unit with the ability to respond to national and local differences and opportunities. The traditional *global* company has managed operations by tightly controlling its worldwide subsidiaries through centralization. Today's companies, as already pointed out, must be local *and* global, that is, *transnational.* The transnational company must operate efficiently and economically through global-scale operations. It must be able to respond to both national and local differences, retaining local flexibility while achieving global integration. The innovative company that can transfer knowledge quickly and efficiently by linking operations to each other will survive. Never before has the design of the information system been so critical to the success of the transnational company. Information processing and technology transfer systems between parent and subsidiary and among the subsidiaries must be flexible and shared. Companies that can develop this transnational organizational capability will have the key to long-term success.

Forms of Organization

Worldwide competitive pressures have recently forced many MNCs into structural reorganizations. Many mixed organizational formats have emerged (e.g., Sony and Unilever), and the traditional matrix organization is used by some. Nevertheless, we distinguish four separate MNC organizational forms in order to get a clearer picture of the information needs involved. The four basic forms of organization used by MNCs are (1) the international division or international department, (2) a grouping by product line, (3) a grouping by geographic area, and (4) the global matrix organization. The *international division* separates foreign operations from domestic operations. The international division is usually evaluated as an independent operation and compared with domestic divisions. Hercules, Inc., Quaker Oats, 3M Company, and Microsoft are all examples of corporations that originally used this form to organize their international operations.

Organization by product line results in the integration of domestic and foreign operations and the evaluation of product line based on worldwide results. This form is used when the product line varies and there is need for product knowledge and expertise. PepsiCo, with such diverse product lines as beverages (Pepsi) and restaurants (Pizza Hut, Taco Bell, and KFC), uses the product line form of organization.

---

[1]John A. Byrne and Kathleen Kerwin, with Amy Cortese and Paula Dwyer, "Borderless Management," *Business Week*, May 23, 1994, pp. 24–26.

Geographic organization separates operations into geographic areas (North America, Europe, etc.). This form is appropriate when country or regional expertise is needed to address issues such as government policies or local consumer behavior patterns. It is used by companies that have relatively simple and stable product lines, for example, chocolate. Nestlé, the Swiss chocolate company, is an example of an MNC organized by geographic area. This structure is appropriate for Nestlé because chocolate is a stable product.

The *global matrix organization* blends two or more of the forms just discussed (e.g., the general manager of a French subsidiary will report to the vice president for worldwide product lines and to the vice president for Europe). Dow Chemical uses the matrix organization to avoid the problems inherent in either integrating or separating foreign operations. ABB Asea Brown Boveri, the Swedish/Swiss electrical engineering MNC, believes in matrix management because it "provides decision makers in the organization with a richer flow of information . . ."[2] Exhibit 8–2 provides a diagram of each MNC organization form.

How do these various forms of organization affect the MNC information system? The form of organization affects the direction of the information *flow,* not the information itself, that is reported by the information system. In all cases information about foreign operations is collected, processed, and reported within the overall MNC system.

With the international division, information flows from subsidiaries to the VP of the international division. In MNCs organized by product line, information flows from subsidiaries to the VP of the product line. When MNCs are geographically organized, the subsidiary information is collected within a geographic area and then sent to headquarters. With the matrix form, information flows in two directions: for example, from the subsidiary to the geographic location headquarters, say, Asia, and also by product line to MNC headquarters.

Attitudes, Organization, and Control

The organizational structure and control functions of the MNC differ depending on the attitude of headquarters management toward multinational business. These attitudes, which are reflected in the MNC's business policies, can be classified as (1) ethnocentric (home-country-oriented), (2) polycentric (host-country-oriented), and (3) geocentric (world-oriented).

An *ethnocentric* MNC thinks that home-country standards are superior and therefore applies them worldwide. A *polycentric* MNC assumes that host-country cultures are different and therefore allows local affiliates to operate quite autonomously (i.e., evaluation and control functions are determined locally). The goal of the *geocentric* approach is to focus on worldwide objectives and to consider foreign subsidiaries as part of a whole. To accomplish this goal, corporate

---

[2]Anonymous, "Big is Back," *The Economist,* London, June 14, 1995, p. 18 (from section under margin bar "Thoroughly Modern Corporations Know No Borders"). © 1995 The Economist Newspaper Group, Inc. Reprinted with permission. Further reproduction prohibited. *www.economist.com*

EXHIBIT 8–2   Diagrams of Various Forms of MNC Organization

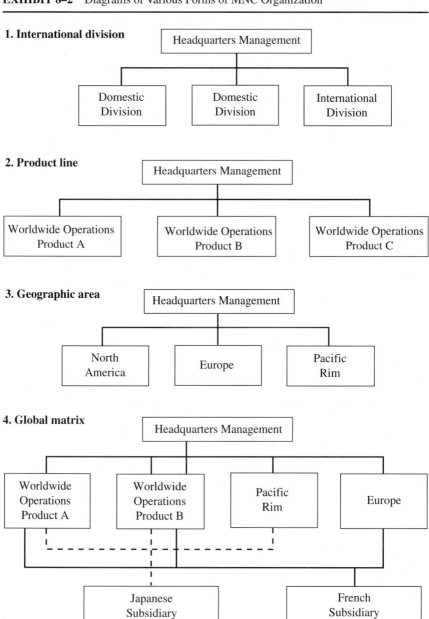

1. International division

Headquarters Management

Domestic Division | Domestic Division | International Division

2. Product line

Headquarters Management

Worldwide Operations Product A | Worldwide Operations Product B | Worldwide Operations Product C

3. Geographic area

Headquarters Management

North America | Europe | Pacific Rim

4. Global matrix

Headquarters Management

Worldwide Operations Product A | Worldwide Operations Product B | Pacific Rim | Europe

Japanese Subsidiary | French Subsidiary

managers try to establish standards for evaluation and control that are both universal and local. The organizational structure of this MNC must facilitate the global coordination of decisions, while at the same time being able to respond to the demands of host governments and the local consumer. Operating with a geocentric attitude is an ideal model not achieved by many MNCs.

Automakers have typically been ethnocentric. Home-country attitudes have prevailed for Fiat from Italy; for Citroen and Renault from France; for BMW from Germany; for Toyota and Nissan from Japan; and for General Motors, Ford, and Chrysler from the United States. However, the auto industry is consolidating worldwide as the 1998 Daimler-Chrysler merger illustrates. Recent acquisitions of Saab (Sweden) by General Motors (U.S.), Jaguar (U.K.) by Ford (U.S.), and Rover (U.K.) by BMW (Germany) will no doubt change the traditional ethnocentric attitude exhibited by automakers (to probably a geocentric one).

Pharmaceutical companies generally exhibit polycentric business strategies. Bayer of Germany wants all consumers from all cultures to think of its aspirin as a local product, just as Roche of Switzerland does with Valium. U.S. pharmaceuticals have established quite a successful presence in Japan and are known as "kakujitsu na kaisha," or reliable company. They have made a long-term commitment to doing business in the Japanese local economy and have built the necessary relationships between customer and supplier. At the same time, they have made an attempt to understand the culture while being open to learning from the Japanese.

ABB Asea Brown Boveri, the Swedish/Swiss electrical giant, operates with a geocentric attitude and is thought of as the "multicultural multinational" by many. ABB consists of more than 1,300 separate companies divided into more than 5,000 profit centers worldwide. Percy Barnevik is the former CEO of ABB. He believes that "purely national companies have little chance of thriving as governments deregulate and as the cost of travel and information plummets. Companies need to keep deep roots in local markets because markets will continue to differ. ABB is a cosmopolitan conglomerate diverse enough to respond to local tastes but united enough to amount to more than the sum of its parts."[3] ABB's coordinating executive committee, charged with supervising the subsidiaries and profit centers, has members from eight countries. In addition, ABB has 500 global managers whose job is "to knit the organization together, to transfer expertise around the world, and to expose the company's leadership to differing perspectives." ABB models multiculturalism and is able to gain firm strategic control of their worldwide operations and manage them in a globally coordinated manner that succeeds in the emerging international economy.

The attitude of headquarters management also affects the location of decision making. If an MNC headquarters allows foreign subsidiaries to make important decisions, the corporation is considered *decentralized*. This attitude is currently

---

[3]Anonymous, "The ABB of Management," *The Economist,* London, January 6, 1996, p. 56. © 1996 The Economist Newspaper Group, Inc. Reprinted with permission. Further reproduction prohibited. *www.economist.com*

the most prevalent among MNC managers who strive for global diversity. Many European and American multinationals have well-established networks of fairly independent and self-sufficient national subsidiaries. Foreign subsidiaries are granted a great deal of autonomy, and therefore subsidiary managers must have information to plan, control, and evaluate their own operations at the local level. These information needs must be built into each subsidiary's accounting information system. At the same time, headquarters management also needs information about the subsidiaries to plan, control, evaluate, and coordinate on a global level. This strategy, and the organizational structure that supports it, makes it difficult to design a system that is able to coordinate and control these worldwide operations, while still responding to global forces.

If decision-making authority rests with headquarters, an MNC is said to be *centralized.* MNCs generally do not make all decisions at one location but aim for a collaborative approach between headquarters and other levels. Many Japanese companies centralize operations in Japan, which allows them to respond to opportunities presented by changing global forces (e.g., movements in exchange rates). An MNC may centralize functions considered critical for success and decentralize those that are less critical. For example, IBM and Nestlé centralize their research and development activities, because headquarters feels R&D is critical to the company's long-run success and wants to maintain tight control over it. However, these companies take a more decentralized approach to their foreign operating subsidiaries, because the success of each one is not as critical to the long-run success of the MNC as a whole.

COMMUNICATION PROBLEMS IN MNCS

Differences in Measurement and Disclosure Practices

As discussed in Chapters 1 through 7, accounting measurement, disclosure, and reporting practices vary a great deal across geographic boundaries. In many countries accounting systems are not well developed, and reporting practices are not as defined as those in the United States. However, for effective control an MNC needs an internal reporting system with standardized, consistent, and uniform accounting principles and practices. Ideally, all subsidiaries should use comparable accounting practices. Assets and liabilities should be valued and reported according to a common plan. Expense recognition should be consistent from year to year (e.g., each subsidiary should use the same depreciation method from year to year). All domestic and foreign managers should understand how headquarters defines the word *profit.* All domestic and foreign subsidiaries of U.S.-based MNCs should use U.S. generally accepted accounting principles for reporting back to corporate headquarters. Consistency and uniformity are particularly important when the information is used to compare one subsidiary's performance to another's.

Differences in cultural, technological, legal, political, and economic heritage pose barriers to communicating uniform information from subsidiaries to the parent company. Simply requiring uniformity does not make these barriers disappear, and simply requiring that certain information be reported on a regular and consistent basis does not guarantee that a subsidiary manager can or will comply. For instance, cultural differences can affect control systems in several ways. Japanese managers, by nature, are far more secretive and less comfortable with disclosing information than are U.S. managers. Japanese managers and employees are quite used to the team approach and naturally use team performance evaluation measures to enhance cooperation. American workers and managers are used to being evaluated as individuals. MNCs cannot simply export control systems and expect them to work in every cultural environment. Then there is the problem of businesses in developing countries not having the technical ability to maintain extensive records or formal accounting reports. For example, it is probably more difficult to acquire standardized information from, say, a subsidiary in Indonesia than from one in Australia. While uniformity is necessary, the system must remain adaptive and flexible to the information needs of both corporate headquarters and the operating subsidiaries. Nevertheless, adaptability is an obstacle to uniformity, and vice versa.

Ease of Communication

Geographic proximity is also a consideration in terms of facilitating the flows of information back and forth between the subsidiaries and headquarters. For example, a U.S.-based MNC would probably find it easier to communicate to a subsidiary in Mexico than one in Chile, simply because the Mexican subsidiary is physically closer. Traditionally, MNCs have transmitted information by mailing paper documents or making phone calls. However, these are giving way to electronic forms of communication (such as e-mail). Electronic communication reduces the amount of time it takes for a parent to communicate with a distant subsidiary (and vice versa) and in many cases makes it nearly instantaneous. Even so, communication across borders can still be difficult. In many MNCs, computer systems are not compatible worldwide. The sheer rate of technological change poses problems for keeping employees up-to-date in using new technology. Cultural barriers can also cause difficulties. Nevertheless, innovations in electronic communication will simplify and improve how MNCs send information around the world.

Financial and Operating Information for Internal Reporting

Many firms equate volumes of reports with good financial control. However, subsidiaries' local management may complain that the volume of required reporting hampers its ability to cope with daily operating problems. In fact, local management is responsible for reporting financial data to the parent *and* operating the subsidiary successfully.

Therefore, the problem is to identify the relevant information that top management needs to maintain the planning and management control systems. This is difficult to achieve. In fact, several studies have shown that MNC headquarters may require a single subsidiary to submit over 200 different financial reports annually. Even with this many reports, there is no assurance that the MNC is well managed.

Goal Congruence

Most major companies in the United States use the profit center or investment center concept for domestic control systems.[4] This approach works relatively well domestically because profit center managers make the major decisions affecting their center's performance. Good decision making ensures good performance evaluation, and good performance evaluation ensures good decision making. The goals are congruent because authority and responsibility are delegated to the same people. Managers are evaluated based on the performance that results from their decisions. Manager performance and profit center performance are linked.

International operations do not lend themselves to management control systems based on a profit center concept. As Chapter 10 explains, foreign subsidiary profits are often somewhat manipulated to facilitate paying the smallest possible amount of income taxes on a worldwide basis. Or by manipulating the prices at which goods are transferred into a country, an MNC can minimize the import duties paid. Each scenario affects a subsidiary's reported profit. Therefore, using the strict profit center concept is inappropriate. In addition, headquarters management must juggle many other environmental variables (e.g., fluctuating exchange rates, inflation, and government controls).

For the profit center idea to work effectively, subsidiary managers must have the authority to make all decisions affecting their profits. Yet many MNCs maintain centralized control over subsidiaries, and many decisions are made at headquarters. Foreign managers may have responsibility for operations, but they do not have the authority to make major decisions affecting their profitability. Such a situation does not enhance goal congruence. Regardless of the situation, some degree of responsibility and authority should be provided to subsidiary managers so that they remain responsive to their local environments. These issues are discussed further in Chapter 9.

CONCLUSION

In this chapter we describe the nature of information systems and the information that managers need to plan, control, evaluate, and coordinate worldwide operations. Planning defines a company's objectives and provides a strategy to

---

[4]For discussion see D. Morse and J. J. Zimmerman, *Management Accounting* (Burr Ridge, IL: Richard D. Irwin, 1997), Chapter 7.

achieve them. Such plans require a management control system as well as a performance evaluation system (the subject of Chapter 9). The management control system should complement the plan so that the goals of the international managers are congruent with the overall goals of the MNC.

REVIEW QUESTIONS

1. How are the objectives of domestic information systems similar to the objectives of MNC information systems?

2. What are the differences among the ethnocentric, polycentric, and geocentric attitudes toward multinational business policies?

3. What is the difference between a global operating strategy versus a multinational operating strategy? Why are these operating strategies no longer effective?

4. What is transnational organizational capability? In what ways does ABB exhibit the characteristics of a transnational company?

5. What problems develop when an MNC tries to establish a uniform system of reporting for its worldwide operations? How can these problems be solved?

6. What demands will the evolution of the transnational corporation place on the planning and control systems of traditional multinational companies?

7. Briefly describe the planning and control implications of the polycentric attitude toward international business, the ethnocentric attitude, the geocentric attitude.

CASES

8–1 Reyab Needs Organization

Reyab is a German diversified, international chemicals and health care group. It sells a wide variety of products and services ranging from pharmaceuticals and crop protection to plastics, specialty chemicals, and imaging technologies. Its major business areas are health care (25% of sales), agriculture (11%), plastics (32%), chemicals (16%), and imaging and photographic products (16%). Most of Reyab's product lines face significant global competition. On the geographic side, Reyab sells products in Europe (55% of sales), North America (28%), Latin America (7%), and Asia/Africa/Australia (10%). Reyab maintains a growth-oriented investment strategy to capitalize on market opportunities while looking to realize additional growth through acquisitions. These strategies are designed to achieve Reyab's strategic objective of being the world's leading integrated chemicals and health care group.

Questions

1. Describe two types of organizational structure that make sense for Reyab. Provide reasoning for your choices.

2. Diagram the organizational structures you described in question 1.

3. What kind of information systems design and control problems does Reyab face given each of the organizational structures you suggested?

8–2 Eltrut Goes Transnational

Eltrut, Inc. is not a new corporation, although it has only been operating internationally for five years. Prior to entering the international marketplace, it was called Eltrut US, and the 20 domestic subsidiaries were organized as decentralized profit centers reporting directly to headquarters.

The five foreign subsidiaries currently report to an international division manager, who reports directly to headquarters. Each subsidiary is labeled a decentralized profit center; however, the international division manager maintains control over each foreign subsidiary manager, and decision making is centralized at headquarters. The foreign subsidiary managers have requested more authority and decision-making responsibility.

Headquarters has decided to reorganize worldwide operations by product line. Its goal is to develop a transnational approach to controlling all subsidiaries, both domestic and foreign. You have been hired to design and implement the new system.

Questions

1. Why were the foreign subsidiaries labeled decentralized profit centers when they were not allowed to act as such? What are the potential problems with a situation like this?

2. As the consultant, what information about this MNC will you need to develop a working information system?

3. Diagram the information flows that will exist for this MNC after the reorganization by product line and the move to "transnationalize."

8–3 Hannaz International

Hannaz International is a U.K. multinational engineering company that has made recent acquisitions in continental Europe and the United States. The company intends to continue to expand by acquiring already existing operations. Products are marketed worldwide and managed geographically by three divisions, but it is the continental Europe–U.S.A. division that is of particular interest to us. Sales of this division have tripled in the past year and account for 25 percent of the company total. The management structure is diagrammed below. The company supports decentralized control. A uniform planning and control system is applied throughout the group, and a finance team at headquarters regularly monitors progress reports. (An organization chart is shown below.)

Prior to being acquired by the company just over a year ago, the Swedish operation was a family-owned business. Frederick Gassar was annoyed when the company accounting system was imposed at the time of takeover, but he recognizes its usefulness. He has been told very little about company strategy and has had very little contact with company management. Little information about the other subsidiaries or the potential for joint actions has been given, and Frederick has found himself competing for the same client's work as other group subsidiaries.

Jules Yount, manager of the French operation, has been on board for 18 months. Under the present arrangement, there are no opportunities for him to make presentations to headquarters management, a situation he finds unusual and frustrating. Quarterly meetings with the group finance director emphasize financial performance indicators, and discussions of strategy are confined. Jules has talked with potential target companies, not fully understanding the exact characteristics that headquarters is seeking. Interaction and cooperation with other subsidiaries, even in the same subgroup, are not encouraged.

Florence White's experience in the business spans some 20 years, although she only joined Hannaz International's U.S. operation two years ago, after the takeover. Her subsidiary consistently meets the company's financial targets and therefore she has little communication with the company. She has little understanding of group strategy and cannot operate as a team player. No written feedback on performance is ever provided but Ann Allen, the Continental Europe–USA manager, does visit once in a while and provides verbal feedback.

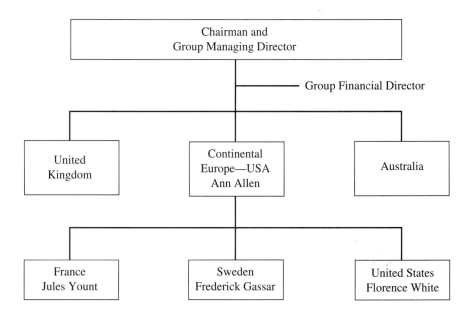

Questions

1. Describe the corporate strategy followed by Hannaz International.

2. Critically evaluate the effectiveness of the management control system in promoting Hannaz's strategy.

3. To what extent is the management style of Hannaz top management creating problems or opportunities relevant to the future success of Hannaz?

ADDITIONAL READINGS

Birkenshaw, J. M., and A. J. Morrison. "Configurations of Strategy and Structure in Subsidiaries of Multinational Corporations." *Journal of International Business Studies* 28, no. 4, 1995, pp. 729–53.

Carr, C., and C. Tomkins. "Context, Culture, and the Role of the Finance Function in Strategic Decisions: A Comparative Analysis of Britain, Germany, the U.S.A., and Japan." *Management Accounting Research* 9, no. 2 (1998), pp. 213–39.

Chen, Y. S. A.; T. Romocki; and G. J. Zuckerman. "Examination of U.S.-Based Japanese Subsidiaries: Evidence of the Transfer of the Japanese Strategic Cost Management." *The International Journal of Accounting* 32, no. 4 (1997), pp. 417–40.

Chow, C. W.; M. D. Shields; and A. Wu. "The Importance of National Culture in the Design of and Preference for Management Controls for Multinational Operations." *Accounting, Organizations, and Society* 12, no. 5/6 (July/August 1999), pp. 441–61.

Dent, J. "Global Competition: Challenges for Management Accounting and Control." *Management Accounting Research* 7, no. 2 (1996), pp. 247–69.

Emmanuel, C.; H. Gernon; and S. J. Gray. "An Approach to Teaching International Management Accounting and Control: Integrating Corporate Strategy, Organizational Structure, and Culture." *Journal of Accounting Education* 16, no. 1 (1998), pp. 65–84.

Goldberg, S. R., and S. W. Martin. "The Effects of the Euro." In *International Accounting and Finance Handbook*. 2nd ed., 1999 Supplement, ed. F. D. S. Choi. New York: John Wiley & Sons, Inc., Chapter 1A pp. 1–21.

Lee, J. Y., and Y. Monden. "An International Comparison of Manufacturing–Friendly Cost Management Systems." *The International Journal of Accounting* 31, no. 2 (1996), pp. 197–212.

Nishimura, A. "Transplanting Japanese Management Accounting and Cultural Relevance." *The International Journal of Accounting* 30, no. 4 (1995), pp. 318–30.

Pedersen, T., and S. Thomsen. "European Patterns of Corporate Ownership: A Twelve-Country Study." *Journal of International Business Studies* 28, no. 4 (1997), pp. 759–78.

9

PERFORMANCE EVALUATION IN MULTINATIONAL CORPORATIONS

LEARNING OBJECTIVES

1. Understand the role that the MNC performance evaluation system plays in relation to MNC strategic planning and control.
2. Know that MNCs use a variety of measures to evaluate their operations.
3. Consider that there are national differences in performance evaluation methods used by MNCs.
4. Be familiar with the issues that complicate multinational performance evaluation.
5. Explain why national performance evaluation systems cannot simply be exported internationally.

Performance evaluation is a critical issue in international accounting. The development of the multinational corporation (MNC) requires an accounting system that records and reports the results of worldwide operations. Headquarters relies on information to evaluate the performance of subsidiaries and managers from all over the world.

This chapter begins with a definition of performance evaluation. We then take a look at various financial measures used by multinationals to evaluate their operations. Some MNCs have begun to use nonfinancial measures to evaluate and enhance their performance. Several issues that must be considered when evaluating domestic and foreign operating environments, subsidiaries, and managers are discussed.

PERFORMANCE EVALUATION DEFINED

Performance evaluation is the periodic review of operations to ensure that the objectives of the enterprise are being accomplished. In other words, it is a report on the success or failure of an operation. A corporation's performance evaluation system is part of its financial control system. One reason for performance evaluation is to reward managers for achieving the organization's goals. Corrective actions can also be taken when achievement falls short of the goals. Performance evaluation guides resource allocation decisions within the multinational organization.

FINANCIAL MEASURES USED BY MNCs TO EVALUATE DOMESTIC AND FOREIGN SUBSIDIARIES

MNCs use various measures to evaluate the results of their operations at home and abroad. Studies of U.S.-based MNCs' performance evaluation practices in the 1970s and 1980s consistently reported using three measures more frequently than any others: profit, budgeted profit compared to actual profit, and return on investment (ROI). Exhibit 9–1 compares the results of four similar

EXHIBIT 9–1 Financial Measures Used as Indicators of Subsidiary Performance Evaluation: U.S.-Based MNCs

	Rankings			
Financial Measures	1980[a]	1984[b]	1990[c]	1991[d]
Profit	1	2	1	1
Budget versus actual profit	3	1	2	2
Return on investment	2	3	3	3

[a]SOURCE: Helen Gernon Morsicato, *Currency Translation and Performance Evaluation in Multinationals* (Ann Arbor, Mich.: UMI Research Press, 1980). MNCs surveyed: 70

[b]SOURCE: Wagdy M. Abdallah, *Internal Accountability: An International Emphasis* (Ann Arbor, Mich.: UMI Research Press, 1984). MNCs surveyed: 64

[c]SOURCE: Ahmad Hosseini and Zabihollah Rezaee, "Impact of SFAS No. 52 on Performance Measures of Multinationals," *The International Journal of Accounting* 25, no. 1 (1990), pp. 43–52. MNCs surveyed: 109

[d]SOURCE: Orapin Duangploy and Dahli Gray, "An Empirical Analysis of Current U.S. Practice in Evaluating and Controlling Overseas Operations," *Accounting and Business Research* 21, no. 84 (1991), pp. 299–309. MNCs surveyed: 111

surveys. Although the rankings changed over time, the three most frequently used measures remained the same. However, a recent survey suggests that some changes may have happened in the 1990s. ROI appears to have fallen out of favor for U.S. MNCs, while sales growth and cost reduction have moved to the top of the list.

That same survey also reports on the performance evaluation practices of Canadian, German, Japanese, and British MNCs. Exhibit 9–2 summarizes the top four financial performance evaluation measures used by MNCs from the five countries surveyed. The exhibit shows the universal popularity of profit margin as a performance indicator and the wide use of sales growth and cost reduction. However, some differences based on the nationality of the MNC are also revealed. For example, budget adherence is more popular in the United States and United Kingdom than in the other three countries.

Profitability Measures

A fundamental measure of operating success is profitability. This can be expressed as gross profit, net income, or return on investment (ROI). Gross profit (or operating margin) is the difference between revenues and the cost of products sold or services provided. Net income is the "bottom line" profit figure of an operation. Expressed as a rate of return, ROI relates profitability to invested capital. It is said that since shareholders are profit oriented, managers should be as well. As discussed later in this chapter, profitability measures imply a level of decentralization that does not always exist in multinational operations. Chapter 10 also points out how transfer pricing policies can distort profitability measures. Thus, they must be used with care and should only be used in conjunction with other performance measures.

EXHIBIT 9–2   Top Four Financial Measures Used as Indicators of Performance Evaluation

Financial Measures	United States	Canada	Germany	Japan	United Kingdom
Sales growth	✓	✓	✓	✓	
Cost reduction	✓	✓	✓		✓
Profit margin	✓	✓	✓	✓	✓
Budget adherence	✓				✓
Goal attainment		✓		✓	✓
Net income			✓	✓	

SOURCE: Exhibit adapted from S. C. Borkowski, "International Managerial Performance Evaluation: A Five Country Comparison," *Journal of International Business Studies,* Third Quarter 1999, pp. 533–55 with permission.

Sales Growth and Cost Reduction

The ability to reach customers is vital to a company's long-run success. Customer acceptance of a company's products or services translates directly into the sales (or revenue) figure. Sales growth may also indicate increased market share.

Cost reduction intensified in the 1990s in response to increased competition brought on by the globalization of product and services markets. Most MNCs reengineered their businesses to improve efficiencies and many spun off peripheral activities in order to focus on their so-called "core competencies." Outsourcing such functions as accounting and information technology were other cost reduction moves.

Of course, sales growth and cost reductions should also improve profitability, as discussed before.

Budgets as a Success Indicator

For some time, budgeting has been accepted as a management tool for controlling operations and forecasting future operations of domestic companies. One purpose of the budget is to clearly set out the objectives of the entity. A budget generally provides a forecast and a means of comparing the actual results of operations to the budget. This comparison produces variances that can be analyzed to evaluate performance and improve the efficiency of future operations.

When a budget is used for a foreign subsidiary, the budget should be developed by that subsidiary. The experience of the local manager is extremely important, in that it produces a deep knowledge of the specific business situation. Thus, the subsidiary manager should fully participate in establishing the subsidiary's goals and in developing its budget. A budget developed on this level will help control the operations and make achievement of goals possible. This budget can be used by the local manager on a daily basis.

Budgeting gives local managers the opportunity to set their own performance standards. In international operations top management is not as familiar with what the standards should be. Headquarters must rely to a greater extent on good local or regional budgets, which help facilitate the strategic planning process.

The subsidiaries' budgets are approved at the parent-company level and often require the endorsement of the president and/or the board of directors. Presumably, headquarters uses the budget to consider the circumstances peculiar to each subsidiary. All of this should ensure a two-way flow of communication between the subsidiary and headquarters which, in turn, will improve the overall budgeting process.

However, preparation of the budget at the local level is not always an easy task. Local managers have different degrees of budgeting expertise. Local customs and norms may affect the budgeting process and are likely to affect the degree of its acceptance and usefulness. Implementation of a system is also difficult due to a lack of familiarity with the technique on the part of local employees of foreign subsidiaries. Budgeting may be a more critical performance evaluation tool for international operations than for domestic ones.

Headquarters uses each foreign subsidiary's budget to develop a worldwide, companywide forecast. Headquarters' analyses are based upon a wide spectrum of knowledge, including knowledge of possible environmental, objective, and strategy changes at the international level. At this headquarters level, profit and return on investment provide the information necessary to assess worldwide profitability and its success or failure. Budgeted information is used more frequently to assess the individual subsidiaries' performances rather than the overall performance of the MNC.

NONFINANCIAL MEASURES USED TO EVALUATE AND ENHANCE MNC PERFORMANCE

A 1995 research report issued by The Conference Board reported that a growing number of major international corporations are using the nonfinancial measures listed in Exhibit 9–3 to capture their firms' potential for future performance. These key measures help transnational companies identify, value, and communicate certain "intangible" assets that do not lend themselves to traditional measurement techniques. The "intangibles" are used internally in a systematic and continuous process for performance measurement and improvement. These companies found traditional financial measures to (1) be too historical, (2) lack predictive behavior, (3) reward the wrong behavior, (4) focus on inputs, not outputs, (5) reflect functions, not cross-functional processes, and (6) give inadequate consideration to hard-to-quantify resources such as intellectual capital. The nonfinancial measures are not meant to replace, but to enhance, the more traditional financial measures discussed previously. The participants expect that using the kind of nonfinancial measures listed in Exhibit 9–3 will lead to increased profitability.

EXHIBIT 9–3   Nonfinancial Measures Used to Evaluate and Enhance
MNC Performance

Quality of output
Customer satisfaction/retention
Employee training
Research and development
Investment and productivity
New product development
Market growth/success
Environmental competitiveness

SOURCE: "Challenging Traditional Measures of Performance," *Deloitte & Touche Review,* August 7, 1995, pp. 1–2.

ISSUES TO CONSIDER WHEN DEVELOPING MNC EVALUATION SYSTEMS

Separating Manager Performance from Subsidiary Performance

Many managerial accountants advocate making a distinction between the performance of the subsidiary manager and that of the subsidiary itself. In practice, MNCs report that they do not make a distinction between the evaluation of the manager and the subsidiary. Surveys continue to show that MNCs use the same measures to evaluate the performance of the manager as that of the foreign subsidiary.

Responsibility reporting as an accounting system traces costs, revenues, assets, and liabilities to the individual manager who is responsible for them. It follows that a manager who has the ability to control the results of operations should be evaluated on the basis of the results over which she or he has control. This system has been widely implemented in U.S. domestic operations and has proven to be generally effective as an evaluation tool. However, the very nature of international operations does not lend itself to effectively implementing a responsibility reporting system in MNCs.

MNC headquarters manages from a worldwide perspective and allocates costs and sets transfer prices to optimize companywide profits and to facilitate worldwide cash flows. (Chapter 10 focuses on transfer prices and taxation.) Therefore, it is naive to evaluate the operating performance of foreign subsidiary managers without first considering all the possible uncontrollable costs that could be allocated to their operations (i.e., royalties, interest, taxes, and exchange gains and losses).

For these reasons, evaluating a manager's performance should be separate from judging the subsidiary as an investment. The manager's evaluation should involve a degree of subjectivity that considers the uniqueness of the subsidiary, environmental peculiarities, actions of the host government, and specific goals of the manager being evaluated. If managers are delegated responsibility for results that are beyond their control, it may lead to behavior that is not in line with headquarters' goals.

Evaluating managers in their local currency before allocation of costs over which they have no direct control is ideal, although somewhat impractical because headquarters usually prefers information translated to the parent currency. Objective measures of performance, profit, and ROI may then be used effectively by headquarters to judge the subsidiary as an investment.

Treating Foreign Subsidiaries as Profit Centers

Profit centers located internationally do not operate in a uniform environment. They operate in environments with different inflation rates and different economic, political, cultural, and technological conditions. Top management is not likely to understand all of the peculiarities of each environment; therefore, it will have trouble evaluating the manager's performance. For these reasons, the profit center concept is less useful when applied to foreign subsidiaries than when applied to domestic subsidiaries. Therefore, it is less successful as a performance indicator.

MNCs also integrate and coordinate operations globally, and it becomes difficult under these circumstances to recognize a particular subsidiary's contribution. The subsidiary manager is not directly responsible for all of the subsidiary's activities. Subsidiaries of an MNC are not independent, and although some control may be decentralized, many major decisions affecting both worldwide profit and individual subsidiary profit are made at headquarters for worldwide efficiency in operations.

Transfer pricing policy (see Chapter 10) in the MNC is not compatible with the profit center concept. A transfer price is a charge for goods exchanged between subsidiaries of the same company. Transfer prices in domestic profit centers are usually set with the objective of maintaining equity between the independent subsidiaries. Transfer prices are set *internationally* for many reasons, which do not necessarily include equity among subsidiaries. These reasons include taxes, tariffs, fluctuating currencies, inflation, economic restrictions on fund transfers, and political instabilities.

Even so, local managers and subsidiaries of MNCs are often evaluated like profit centers. Yet central coordination of the MNC makes it difficult to evaluate the local managers' performance. These managers do not make many of the important decisions affecting their operations. It is also difficult to evaluate how effectively a subsidiary is using its resources.

The responsibility reporting concept implies that the manager and the local entity should be evaluated separately. Separating the two enables each to be judged according to its contribution to global optimization.

Currency Choice

The accounting records and financial statements of a foreign subsidiary are generally maintained in the subsidiary's local currency. Therefore, an issue arises as to which currency should be used to evaluate the performance of the subsidiary and its manager. Two logical candidates are the subsidiary's local currency or the parent's home currency.

We recommend using local currency information. In our view, this results in far more meaningful and valid comparisons of past, present, and future operations of a subsidiary. Using the local currency is consistent with isolating and weighing the environmental peculiarities of each operating environment. Such information relates to local conditions and it avoids the distortions that result from fluctuating exchange rates. A local currency perspective also applies to evaluating the foreign manager. As noted earlier, managers should be evaluated as meeting primary goals in the local currency (e.g., annual profits and sales forecasts, meeting projected production levels, managing the effects of inflation, and managing employees). European MNCs mostly report a preference for local currency procedures.

Nevertheless, there is a problem with universally using local currency information for evaluating foreign operations. Decision making by boards of directors and management headquarters are usually based on the parent's home currency. If one level of management bases decisions on home currency information and another on local currency information, problems with goal congruency and optimization of resources may result. Most U.S. MNCs prefer U.S. dollar measures over local currency measures. They want their managers worldwide to "keep their eyes" on the U.S. dollar, think in dollar terms, and manage toward dollar results. After all, they have U.S. investors who expect U.S.-dollar dividends, they finance their operations abroad from a U.S.-dollar risk management perspective, and they prepare their consolidated financial statements in U.S. dollars.

If the parent's home currency is used for performance evaluation, then foreign currency translation methods (Chapter 6) must be employed. Studies have shown that most U.S. MNCs use the same method to translate for internal reporting purposes (managerial accounting) that they use for external reporting purposes (financial accounting). As discussed in Chapter 6, the Financial Accounting Standards Board has issued *Statement 52,* "Foreign Currency Translation," for external reporting purposes. Assuming that we are dealing with *autonomous* subsidiaries, we use the year-end exchange rate (current rate) to translate the balance sheet and average-for-the-year rate to translate the income statement. The result is that operating relationships and income statement ratios remain intact throughout the translation process. Users of this information can then see in dollars the same relationships that existed in the currency where the revenues were earned and expenses were incurred. Notice in Exhibit 9–4, for example, that the ratio of total debt to total assets is the same in local currency (LC 1100 ÷ LC 1500 = 73 percent) as it is in U.S. dollars ($550 ÷ $750 = 73 percent).

EXHIBIT 9–4   Effect of Translation on Balance Sheet Accounts

	Local Currency	Current Rate	U.S. Dollars
Cash	LC 300	1 LC = $0.50	$150
Inventory	400		200
Building and land	800		400
	LC 1,500		$750
Current liabilities	LC 300	1 LC = $0.50	$150
Long-term debt	800		400
Stockholder's equity	400		200
	LC 1,500		$750

Therefore, for autonomous subsidiaries it can be assumed that the information used by U.S. MNCs to evaluate foreign subsidiaries and their managers is also translated at the current exchange rate in effect at the time of translation. This method provides translated financial statements that are similar to local currency financial statements, consistent with a local currency perspective.

CONCLUSION

Multinational corporations need flexible performance evaluation models capable of incorporating factors peculiar to an MNC for the separate evaluation of subsidiary and manager. This chapter has identified financial and nonfinancial measures currently being used in MNC performance evaluation systems. Explanations of these measures have also noted some of their shortcomings, suggesting why care should be taken in employing them. Because performance evaluation systems used by MNCs have international economic impact, these systems should be under constant examination, and improvements should be made continuously.

REVIEW QUESTIONS

1. What role does the MNC performance evaluation system play in relation to strategic planning and control? (Review Chapter 8.)

2. Why should financial comparisons of subsidiaries operating in different countries be made cautiously?

3. Why are MNCs beginning to use nonfinancial measures as indicators of performance? What is it about the nonfinancial measures listed in Exhibit 9–3 that makes them difficult to quantify?

4. Budgeting is thought to be a more useful and critical tool for evaluating foreign subsidiary managers than domestic managers. Describe a "good" budgeting process and explain why it works in the international environment.

5. What are some national differences in performance evaluation methods used by MNCs?

6. What are the alternatives to using translated information when judging foreign subsidiaries?

7. You are the CFO (chief financial officer) of an MNC headquartered in the United Kingdom. You are thinking about how convoluted the issues are that influence the internal performance evaluation of your subsidiaries and their managers. Make a list of the issues and be ready to discuss them.

CASES

9–1 Whose Responsibility?

Big Fish International (BFI) has operations in several countries around the world. One of BFI's foreign subsidiaries, Little Trout Ltd. (LTL), provides the following income statement covering its operations for the most recent year. It is stated in Pesaros (P), LTL's local currency.

Sales revenue	P630,000
Cost of goods sold	(319,000)
Gross profit	P311,000
Selling and administrative expenses	(236,000)
Interest expense	(15,000)
Pretax income	P60,000
Income tax expense	(34,000)
Net income	P26,000

You wish to prepare a performance report of LTL's manager, reflecting those aspects under her control. Some of BFI's activities are coordinated across countries, and some functions are centrally managed at BFI headquarters. You learn the following additional information:

1. Financing decisions and tax planning are centralized at corporate headquarters. Each subsidiary is allocated a portion of BFI's overall interest expense.

2. Similarly, each subsidiary is charged an administrative fee for its "fair share" of BFI's corporate overhead. LTL's charge of P28,000 is included in selling and administrative expenses.

3. Included in LTL's sales revenue is P120,000 worth of items sold to another of BFI's subsidiaries. BFI instructed LTL to invoice the sale at 25 percent below market prices.

4. Local labor laws in LTL's country require overtime payments when employees work more than 32 hours per week. Overtime charges amounting to P31,000 are included in selling and administrative expenses.

Questions

1. Which items are relevant in evaluating the performance of LTL's manager?

2. Prepare a performance report for the manager of LTL.

3. How does your performance report change if you are evaluating LTL as a subsidiary operating unit of BFI?

9–2 At the Top or at the Bottom?

You are the manager of operations in the Republic of Alkura. You are in the United States attending a meeting of operating managers from all over the world. Earlier in the meeting, you were praised because your operation's sales and income growth were higher than those of every other manager for the second year in a row. An overhead transparency of your three-year sales and income showed the following. All amounts are stated in your local currency, the Kuren (K).

	2001	2000	1999
Sales	K 15,000,000	K 11,200,000	K 10,000,000
Income	K 1,410,000	K 1,080,000	K 850,000

The meeting now turns to comparing operations stated in U.S. dollars. All of a sudden, yours are at the bottom. In fact, you look particularly bad when compared to last year's sales and income growth. You feel embarrassed, angry, and confused.

Questions

1. What are your sales and income growth amounts (this year and last year) stated in Kurens?

2. What are your sales and income growth amounts (this year and last year) stated in U.S. dollars? Assume the following exchange rates:

	2001	2000	1999
Kurens/$1	15	11	12

3. Why do the results in Kurens and dollars look so different?

4. Is it better to evaluate you in Kurens or in dollars? Why?

9–3 MJ International

MJ International (MJI) is a U.S. multinational corporation with manufacturing subsidiaries in Asia, Europe, and North and South America. Traditionally, MJI has used a variety of financial measures to evaluate the performance of these manufacturing subsidiaries and their managers. The Asian managers have asked for a change because they feel that the financial measures do not capture how effectively they operate their manufacturing facilities. MJI's top management group has always had an open door policy when it comes to managing, and they are carefully listening to the managers from China, South Korea, Japan, and Taiwan. These managers want alternatives to ROI.

Questions

1. Can you effectively separate the performance evaluation of the manufacturing subsidiary from the evaluation of its manager? Discuss.

2. Are there any nonfinancial measures that MJI can use?

3. What problems might develop in trying to quantify nonfinancial measures of performance evaluation?

ADDITIONAL READINGS

Borkowski, S. C. "International Managerial Performance Evaluation: A Five Country Comparison." *Journal of International Business Studies* 30, no. 3 (Third Quarter 1999), pp. 533–55.

Chow, C. W.; Y. Kato; and K. A. Merchant. "The Use of Organizational Controls and Their Effects on Data Manipulation and Management Myopia: A Japan vs. U.S. Comparison." *Accounting, Organizations, and Society* 21, no. 2/3 (February/April 1996), pp. 175–92.

Chow, C. W.; M. D. Shields; and A. Wu. "The Importance of National Culture in the Design of and Preference for Management Controls for Multinational Operations." *Accounting, Organizations, and Society* 24, no. 5/6 (July/August 1999), pp. 441–61.

Indjejkian, R. I. "Performance Evaluation and Compensation Research: An Agency Perspective." *Accounting Horizons* 13, no. 2 (June 1999), pp. 147–57.

Lal, M.; A. S. Dunk; and G. D. Smith. "The Propensity of Managers to Create Budgetary Slack: A Cross-National Re-examination using Random Sampling." *The International Journal of Accounting* 31, no. 4 (1996), pp. 483–96.

Lau, C. M., and J. J. Tan. "The Impact of Budget Emphasis, Participation, and Task Difficulty on Managerial Performance: A Cross-Cultural Study of the Financial Services Sector." *Management Accounting Research* 9, no. 2 (June 1998), pp. 163–83.

Merchant, K. A.; C. W. Chow; and A. Wu. "Measurement, Evaluation, and Reward of Profit Center Managers: A Cross-Cultural Field Study." *Accounting, Organizations, and Society* 20, no. 7/8 (October/November 1995), pp. 619–38.

Mezias, S. J. et al. "Dynamic Performance Evaluation Systems for a Global World: The Complexities to Come." Chapter 13A in *International Accounting and Finance Handbook*. 2nd ed., ed. F. D. S. Choi. New York: John Wiley & Sons, 1999 Supplement.

Salter, S. "Managerial Accounting." Chapter 21 in *Comparative International Accounting*. 5th ed., eds. C. Nobes and R. Parker. London: Prentice Hall Europe, 1998.

Wijewardena, H., and A. De Zoysa. "A Comparative Analysis of Management Accounting Practices in Australia and Japan: An Empirical Investigation." *The International Journal of Accounting* 34, no. 1 (1999), pp. 49–70.

10

INTERNATIONAL TAXATION AND MULTINATIONAL TRANSFER PRICING

LEARNING OBJECTIVES

1. Be able to define a number of tax incentives: tax credit, tax treaty, tax haven, tax exemption, and the deferral principle.

2. Understand why the international harmonization of taxation would simplify business decision making.

3. Identify transfer pricing as the leading international tax issue and understand why.

4. Realize that transfer pricing is viewed as a compliance exercise in some MNCs, while in others, it is a part of the strategic planning process.

5. Be aware that national taxing authorities in both developed and emerging markets are paying increased attention to transfer pricing methods and their documentation.

We have established that the purpose of a management control system is to accomplish the objectives of the strategic plan. The control system is designed to communicate information that enhances goal congruence and that provides the basis for decision making throughout all levels of the multinational corporation (MNC).

The MNC must deal with two additional complicating variables that do not affect domestic corporations. The first is international taxation and its pervasive influence on MNC operations. The second is transfer pricing, the most important international tax issue facing MNCs. This chapter discusses some of the available strategies that MNCs use to minimize their worldwide tax liability. The objectives of MNC transfer pricing and factors considered in shaping the MNC transfer pricing policy are also discussed. The transfer price selected for the pricing of goods and services that move across national borders can have a significant impact on the MNC's worldwide tax liability.

INTERNATIONAL TAXATION—SELECTED TOPICS

Multinational companies say the job of preparing their taxes is incredibly complex and expensive. Citigroup's 1998 return "exceeded 30,000 pages in length, including computations for more than 2,000 companies located in 50 states and 200 countries,"[1] says Denise Strain, general tax counsel of its Citicorp unit.

International taxation has a pervasive effect on multinationals and, therefore, enters into most management decisions. Taxation affects where an MNC invests, how it markets its products, what form of business organization it selects, when and where to remit cash, how to finance, and the choice of a transfer price.

Tax systems are used worldwide to affect economic policy, social issues, and the political scene; they are as varied as the nations developing them. International taxation is extremely complex and constantly changing. As tax treaties, agreements, laws, and regulations change, the multinational tax network must be reviewed and reworked to maintain relative worldwide advantages.

The gradual integration of world economies, globalization, is resulting in a freer flow of labor and capital than the world has seen previously. This means that labor and capital can move from high-tax countries to low-tax ones if they decide to do so. Exhibit 10–1 shows us that the corporate income tax levied by the nations (industrialized and less industrialized) of the world varies dramatically. So nations have to constantly rethink and review their taxing policies to retain companies within their borders. International competition for labor and capital is expected to eventually result in a convergence of corporate tax rates.

Globalization makes it hard to decide where a company should pay tax, regardless of where its headquarters are or where it chooses to incorporate. Multinational corporations design their products in one country, manufacture them in another, and then sell them all over the world. Tax planning is perfectly legal and as long as there are disparities in the tax rates there is room for this type of planning. More is said about tax planning strategies in a later section and also when we discuss transfer pricing.

---

[1]Anonymous, "Tax Report," *The Wall Street Journal* (July 21, 1999), p. 1.

EXHIBIT 10–1   Corporate Income Tax Rates, Top Rates, %

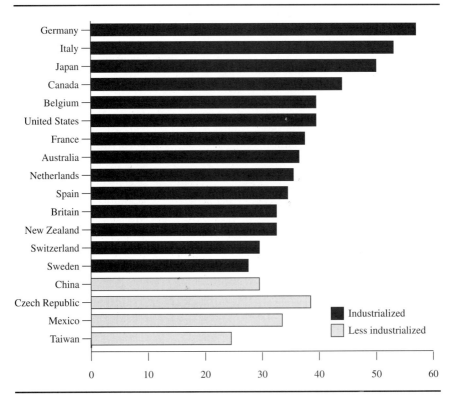

Philosophy of Taxation

A country may follow the territorial principle that income earned outside its domestic boundaries is not taxed. Other nations follow the worldwide principle that they have the right to tax income earned outside their boundaries when earned by an entity based in the country. The worldwide principle results in double taxation because the income is taxed where earned and then again to the parent company.

However, double taxation is mitigated by tax credits, tax treaties, tax havens, the "deferral principle," and tax exemption. A *tax credit* allows an entity to reduce the taxes paid to the domestic government by the amount of taxes paid to the foreign government. A credit is a direct reduction of the tax liability and reduces double taxation to a certain extent. A *tax treaty* between nations establishes what items of income will or will not be taxed by the authorities of the country where the income is earned. Exhibit 10–2 provides a listing of U.S. tax treaty countries. A *tax haven* is a country with an exceptionally low, or even no, income tax. It

---

EXHIBIT 10–2   Selected U.S. Tax Treaty Countries

Argentina	Hungary	Norway
Aruba	Iceland	Pakistan
Australia	India	Philippines
Austria	Indonesia	Poland
Bangladesh	Ireland	Portugal
Barbados	Israel	Romania
Belgium	Italy	Russian Federation
Bermuda	Jamaica	Slovak Republic
Canada	Japan	South Africa
China	Korea	Spain
Cyprus	Luxembourg	Sri Lanka
Czech Republic	Malta	Sweden
Denmark	Mexico	Switzerland
Egypt	Morocco	Thailand
Finland	Netherlands	Trinidad & Tobago
France	Netherlands Antilles	Tunisia
Germany	New Zealand	United Arab Republic
Greece	Nigeria	United Kingdom

SOURCE: Jack R. Fay and Judson P. Stryker, "An Update on Foreign Taxes," *The CPA Journal,* October 1995, pp. 28–29 and 50–52.

generally offers a company the right to earn or transfer income within its borders and pay little or no tax. Tax havens are normally used by MNCs to shift income from a country with a high tax rate to the tax haven. The Isle of Man, a British seaside resort, is just such a tax haven. It is a self-ruling dependency with enough autonomy to set its own tax rates on corporations and individuals, both currently at no more than 20 percent. Over the past 20 years, financial services businesses have located their offices on, and moved money to, this island. The Isle of Man economy is growing twice as fast as that of Great Britain. The *deferral principle* works so that parent companies are not taxed on foreign source income until they actually receive a dividend. A *tax exemption* allows certain corporations to pay no tax on certain income.

Many MNCs were avoiding U.S. taxation by combining the tax deferral principle with the advantage of a tax haven and repatriating dividends to the tax haven instead of to the United States. As a result, the Controlled Foreign Corporation (CFC) rules were passed by Congress. These rules tax U.S. shareholders on CFC income when it is earned, regardless of when it is received, and thus eliminate the ability to avoid taxes in the manner described.

Congress also created the Foreign Sales Corporation (FSC) to encourage foreign sales by exporters. Part of the taxable income of the FSC is exempt from U.S. income tax. There are more than 5000 FSCs used by U.S. corporations. The

EXHIBIT 10–3   Ten Best-known EU Tax Incentives

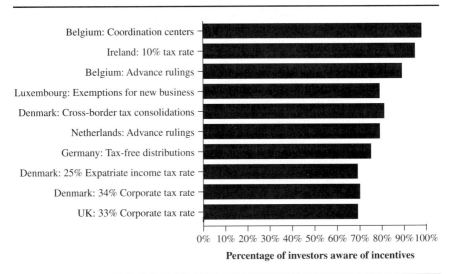

SOURCE: "Survey Examines Tax Incentives in EU Countries," *Deloitte & Touche Review,* May 27, 1996, p. 5.

requirements for qualifying as an FSC are extremely complex and beyond the scope of this book.

Tax rates and incentive plans are important factors to consider when choosing where to invest. In 1996 Deloitte Touche Tohmatsu International, an international public accounting firm, conducted a survey to investigate the role of favorable tax rules in decisions to invest in European Union (EU) countries. About 100 multinational companies from Europe, the United States, Canada, Hong Kong, and Japan responded.

Eighty percent of the companies reported that EU tax issues influence investment decisions. However, economic incentives were considered more important than tax incentives by 51 percent of the respondents. Political and economic stability, geographic location, infrastructure, a skilled workforce, and a strong currency were also considered important. Low tax rates are the most popular tax incentive. Forty-two beneficial tax rules available in the EU countries were identified in the survey; however, only half of these incentives were known to over 50 percent of the companies that had invested in the country that offered the incentive. Exhibit 10–3 lists the 10 best-known tax incentives by country offering the incentive. Notice that Belgium, Ireland, Denmark, and Luxembourg offer the best-known incentives.

In prior chapters, we discussed the diversity in financial reporting practices throughout the world and efforts to harmonize these practices. Now we see a tremendous amount of global diversity in tax philosophy, policies, incentives, and rates. The international harmonization of taxation would certainly simplify business decision making. The European Union is attempting to accomplish this as the 15 member countries become a single market. International tax reform is a topic on many multinational company board of directors' agendas.

MNC Tax Avoidance

Tax avoidance is the legal reduction of one's tax liability and is accomplished by tax planning. Tax avoidance enters into most managerial decisions and, therefore, plays a role in the planning process, the management control system, and performance evaluation. A *tax-planning information system* that attempts to accomplish worldwide tax minimization and tax avoidance should incorporate the following procedures: (1) stating the objectives of tax planning in MNC operations, (2) delegating responsibilities for tax planning to both headquarters and subsidiaries, (3) determining what operations are affected by tax considerations and how they are affected, (4) communicating necessary information to the tax planners and decision makers, and (5) evaluating the impact tax considerations have on an MNC strategic plan and management control system.

OBJECTIVES OF TRANSFER PRICING

The need for determining a transfer price arises when goods or services are exchanged between organizational units of the same company (e.g., charges for administrative and managerial services, royalties for intangible rights, transfers of finished goods for resale, and charges for technical services). A transfer price is a substitute for a market price. It is used when one subsidiary of a corporation sells to another. The transfer pricing system places a monetary value on intracompany exchanges that occur between operating units. This price is recorded by the seller as revenue and by the buyer as cost.

Example 1.   Subsidiary A sells 1,000 units of product X to subsidiary B for $7 per unit. The $7 selling price is the *transfer price.*

It is generally agreed that the transfer pricing system for a *domestic* corporation should accomplish certain objectives including (1) the communication of information resulting in desirable decision making by managers, (2) providing a report of divisional profits that reasonably measures the economic performance of the division, and (3) enhancing goal congruence.

Achieving these objectives may be difficult. If a manager makes a decision that increases the profit of his/her particular profit center, it may affect the profits of a competing profit center negatively. An example of such a decision is charging an inflated transfer price for goods transferred to a division. The first profit center will show increased sales and a higher profit; however, the second profit center will show increased cost of purchases and a lower profit.

Example 2.   Subsidiary A sells 1,000 units of product X to subsidiary B for $8 per unit. The normal market price is $6 per unit. Subsidiary A shows increased sales of $2 per unit and a higher profit. Subsidiary B shows that cost of goods sold has increased by $2 per unit and therefore has a lower profit.

Those who develop domestic internal transfer pricing systems are aware of this potential dilemma and attempt to create a system that motivates managers not to make undesirable decisions. Ideally, a manager acts in the best interests of the company as a whole, even at the expense of the reported profits of his/her own division. To effect this ideal behavior, the system of performance evaluation must reward a manager who chooses companywide goal congruence over divisional performance.

OBJECTIVES OF INTERNATIONAL TRANSFER PRICING

Developing an MNC transfer pricing system is far more complex than developing a domestic system. As with the *domestic* corporation, an MNC pricing system should result in managers making desirable decisions that enhance goal congruence. Providing a reasonable measure of a subsidiary's economic performance is often an irrelevant transfer pricing objective when dealing with an MNC. An MNC pricing system must attempt to meet the objectives of the strategic plan, the management control system, and the system of performance evaluation. (See Chapters 8 and 9 for a discussion of these objectives.) The international transfer pricing system must also attempt to accomplish objectives that are irrelevant in a purely domestic operation.

In a study of 82 U.S.-based multinationals, respondents were asked to rank certain transfer pricing objectives. Exhibit 10–4 presents the sample results on this question. Both the primary and top three most important objectives are listed. Most MNCs report having multiple objectives. The exhibit shows that 40 percent of the respondents consider managing the overall tax burden (liability) to be the primary objective of setting transfer prices. However, many other objectives are also reported as being important: maintaining a competitive market position, performance evaluation, motivating managers, goal congruence between the managers and the firm, managing tariffs, and compliance with the tax law.

Ernst & Young, an international accounting firm, surveyed 393 multinational parent companies (99 from the United States) on a variety of international tax and transfer pricing issues. Companies from Australia, Canada, France, Germany, Italy, Japan, Korea, the Netherlands, Sweden, Switzerland, the United Kingdom, and the United States participated in this 1997 survey. The survey looked at factors MNCs consider in setting transfer pricing policies and Exhibit 10–5 reports the results. Notice that for this group of respondents, maximizing operating performance is a main priority for 45 percent. Only 25 percent of the respondents regard optimizing tax arrangements as a main priority. When we compare these results to the results of the prior study of only U.S.-based MNCs, we see that tax

EXHIBIT 10–4   Transfer Pricing Objectives of Sample Firms

Transfer Pricing Objective	Percent Firms Listing as Primary	Percent Firms Listing as One of Three Most Important
Management of overall tax burden	40	28
Maintain competitive market position	21	17
Motivate managers	9	10
Equitable performance evaluation	7	11
Compliance with tax law	7	7
Goal congruence between managers and the firm	5	10
Reflect actual costs/income in consistent manner	5	0
Manage tariffs	4	9
Mitigate cash transfer restrictions	1	4
None specified	1	0
Manage foreign currency exchange	0	2
Minimize inflation risk	0	1
Address social or political concerns	0	1

SOURCE: K. S. Cravens and W. T. Shearon, "An Outcome-Based Assessment of International Transfer Pricing," *The International Journal of Accounting,* 31-4, 1999, pp. 419–43.

EXHIBIT 10–5   Factors Shaping Transfer Pricing Policies

	A Main Priority	Important but Not a Main Priority	Not Very Important	Not Important at All
Maximizing operating performance	45%	29%	22%	4%
Documentation in preparation for audit	25%	48%	21%	6%
Optimizing tax arrangements	25%	51%	20%	4%
Financial efficiencies	24%	48%	22%	6%
Performance incentives	11%	27%	44%	18%

SOURCE: Ernst & Young International, Ltd., *Ernst & Young Transfer Pricing 1997 Global Survey* (1997), p. 10.

minimization is not as high a priority outside the United States as it is to managers operating within the United States.

Worldwide Income Tax Minimization

The transfer pricing system can be used to shift taxable profits from a country with a high tax rate to a country with a lower tax rate; the result is that after taxes the MNC retains more profits. Exhibit 10–1 reports the corporation income tax rates for a variety of countries throughout the world. As you can see, corporate rates vary considerably. Unless the performance evaluation system is compatible with the transfer pricing system, undesirable decision making can result at the subsidiary manager level. If each subsidiary is evaluated as an independent profit center, the transfer pricing policies must be considered when evaluating the manager's performance, or else conflict between subsidiary and MNC goals may result.

Example 3. Subsidiary X operates in Japan, where the tax rate is 50 percent. Subsidiary Y operates in Switzerland with a tax rate of 30 percent. X sells goods to Y at an inflated transfer price of $10 per item. The current market price is $7 per item. Subsidiary X shows a higher profit and is taxed at 50 percent. Subsidiary Y shows a higher cost of goods sold and a lower profit on future sales taxed at 30 percent. These subsidiaries are not practicing worldwide tax minimization. However, this behavior would not be unusual for a Japanese company. Japanese companies prefer to shift profits to Japan, even though the Japanese corporate tax rate is higher. There are political reasons to shift profits to Japan in order to please the government authorities and to gain the cooperation of the local suppliers.

Minimization of Worldwide Import Duties

Transfer prices can reduce tariffs. Import duties are normally applied to intracompany transfers as well as to sales to unaffiliated buyers. If the goods are transferred in at low prices, the resulting tariffs will be lower. This same pricing strategy may be used when a country places a ceiling on the value of goods that may be imported. By valuing at low transfer prices, a subsidiary may be able to import a larger *quantity* of goods and services. If a country had a low tariff on imports, a higher transfer price could be charged.

Tariffs interact with income taxes. Low import duties are often associated with a country with high income tax rates. The opposite may also be found—high import duties with low income tax rates. The MNC must deal with the customs officials and income tax administrators of the importing country and with the income tax administrators of the exporting country. A higher import tariff would result in a lower remaining profit for determining income taxes. The MNC has to evaluate the benefits of a lower (higher) income tax in the importing country against a higher (lower) import tariff as well as the potentially higher (lower) income tax paid by the MNC in the exporting country.

Avoidance of Financial Restrictions

When a foreign government places economic restrictions on MNC operations, transfer prices may mitigate the impact of these national controls. Suppose a country restricts the amount of cash that may leave its boundaries in the form of dividend payments. Setting a high transfer price on goods imported into the country may facilitate the desired movement of cash because the importing subsidiary must remit payment. However, cash transfers are not easily accomplished in a country that watches import and export prices closely.

Some countries allow a tax credit or subsidy based on the value of goods exported. In this case, a high transfer price on exported products is followed by a larger tax credit or higher subsidy. A tax credit of this nature reduces the corresponding tax liability to the host country dollar for dollar and more than offsets the higher taxable income. A subsidy is generally a payment from the government to the subsidiary.

Restrictions may be placed on an MNC by disallowing a foreign subsidiary to deduct certain expenses provided by the parent against taxable income. Common examples include research and development expenses, general and administrative expenses, and royalty fees. By inflating the transfer price of imports to the subsidiary, such expenses may be recovered.

If an MNC desires to show low (high) profitability, high (low) transfer prices on imports to subsidiaries may be used. An MNC may want to appear less profitable to discourage potential competitors from entering the market. Higher profits may cause the subsidiary's employees to demand higher wages or even to request some type of profit-sharing plan. Expropriation (takeover) of highly profitable foreign-owned subsidiaries may also be avoided if they appear less profitable.

Lower transfer prices on imports should improve the subsidiary's financial position. This may be desirable when the MNC wants to finance the foreign subsidiary with funds from a local lender rather than committing its own capital. In this instance, the lender would probably require that the subsidiary have a positive financial condition. Lower transfer prices may also allow the subsidiary to enjoy a competitive edge during its initial stages of growth.

Managing Currency Fluctuations

A country suffering from balance-of-payments problems may decide to devalue its national currency. Losses from such a devaluation may be avoided by using inflated transfer prices to transfer funds from the country to the parent or to some other affiliate.

Balance-of-payments problems often result from an inflationary environment. Inflation erodes the purchasing power of the MNC's monetary assets. Using inflated transfer prices on goods imported to such an environment may offer a timely cash removal method.

Winning Host-Country Government Approval

The manipulation of transfer prices has not gone unnoticed. Generally, there is increased government concern about intracorporate pricing and its effect on reported profits. In an era when an MNC must be concerned about justifying its existence, maintaining positive relations with the host government is a good idea. Continually changing and manipulating transfer prices is not good policy.

Most governments are becoming more sophisticated and aware of the results of using high or low transfer prices. Using unfavorable prices to a country's detriment results in the loss of goodwill. It is beneficial in the long run to develop transfer pricing policies that satisfy the foreign authorities, even though it may mean sacrificing some profits.

In summary, we have discussed several transfer pricing objectives that MNCs must consider and that are not applicable to a purely domestic corporation. Exhibit 10–6 provides a summary of the conditions that make it advisable to use a particular transfer price. Unfortunately, an MNC is usually faced with conditions that appear in both columns of the exhibit.

MNCs may resort to maintaining a separate set of financial information for the foreign governments and another set for headquarters to use in the management control process and the performance evaluation system. Unfortunately, the information provided to the foreign government is often used to evaluate the performance of a subsidiary that has been told to produce a low profit to minimize income taxes. If headquarters overlooks the fact that low profits were due to an unfavorable transfer price, hard feelings between subsidiary managers and headquarters may result. It may also cause subsidiary managers to act undesirably. In

---

EXHIBIT 10–6   Conditions in Subsidiary's Country Inducing High and Low Transfer Prices on Flows between Affiliates and Parent

Conditions Inducing Low Transfer Prices on Flows from Parent and High Transfer Prices on Flows to Parent	*Conditions Inducing High Transfer Prices on Flows from Parent and Low Transfer Prices on Flows to Parent*
High ad valorem tariffs	Local partners
Corporate income tax rate lower than in parent's country	Pressure from workers to obtain greater share of company profit
Significant competition	Political pressure to nationalize or expropriate high-profit foreign firms
Local loans based on financial appearance of subsidiary	Restrictions on profit or dividend remittances
Export subsidy or tax credit on value of exports	Political instability
Lower inflation rate than in parent's country	Substantial tie-in sales agreements
Restrictions (ceilings) in subsidiary's country on the value of products that can be imported	Price of final product controlled by government but based on production cost
	Desire to mask profitability of subsidiary operations to keep competitors out

SOURCE: Jeffrey S. Arpan, *International Intracorporate Pricing: Non-American Systems and Views* (New York: Praeger Publishers, 1972).

the long run, morale problems could develop and destroy the short-run effect of tax minimization.

Transfer pricing is a business as well as a tax issue that should be considered by headquarters when planning. However, transfer pricing is often not considered at the board room level. The Ernst & Young survey, referred to earlier, found that only about 25 percent of MNCs consider transfer pricing as part of the strategic planning process. Others address it after the strategic decisions have been made and treat it as a tax compliance issue rather than as an important strategic issue. This behavior often results in significant tax costs.

SELECTING A TRANSFER PRICE

Selecting a transfer price is a difficult problem for MNCs that are trying to balance the requirements of multiple tax jurisdictions with the demands of their own subsidiaries. The United States set up formal regulations to deal with transfer pricing practices in 1968, making it the first country to address the issue of choice. Then in 1992, the United States began an aggressive enforcement of these regulations and introduced extensive transfer pricing documentation requirements and costly non-negotiable penalties. Since then, Australia, Brazil, Canada, France, Korea, and Mexico have developed their own penalties and documentation requirements in order to protect their own tax bases. Exhibit 10–7 presents the findings from the Ernst & Young study on the number of MNCs that prepare transfer

EXHIBIT 10–7   Countries for Which Transfer Pricing Documentation Has Been Prepared

Country	Number Operating in Country	Number That Have Prepared Documentation	Percent That Have Prepared Documentation
Australia	87	52	61%
Canada	115	66	57%
France	140	64	46%
Germany	181	77	43%
Italy	94	36	38%
Japan	76	39	51%
Netherlands	87	39	45%
Sweden	39	19	49%
Switzerland	38	15	39%
United Kingdom	232	117	50%
United States	265	207	78%

SOURCE: Ernst & Young International, Ltd., *Ernst & Young Transfer Pricing 1997 Global Survey* (1997), p. 12.

pricing documentation given various countries of operation. Notice that a number of MNCs prepare documentation even for countries (such as Italy) that do not yet require such information.

The *Internal Revenue Code* and Transfer Pricing

All multinationals doing business in the United States must consider Section 482 of the *Internal Revenue Code* when pricing intercompany transactions (intracompany transactions from a headquarters' point of view). Section 482 gives the Internal Revenue Service (IRS) the authority to reallocate income and deductions among subsidiaries if it determines that this is necessary to prevent tax evasion, the illegal reduction of taxes, or to clearly reflect the income of the subsidiary. Intercompany sales of goods must appear to be priced at arm's-length market values. In addition, the IRS also scrutinizes the transfer of services, intangibles (such as trademarks, patents, and basic research), and R&D cost sharing arrangements among commonly controlled entities. Being required to use arm's-length transfer prices does not always allow an MNC to pursue the objective of worldwide profit maximization. According to the IRS, the arm's-length principle to be applied is whether unrelated parties with a reasonable level of experience, exercising sound business judgment, would have agreed to the same contractual terms. This principle does not always support the objective of MNC transfer pricing philosophy.

An MNC pursuing tax minimization must be careful to use transfer prices that appear to reflect arm's-length sales to avoid IRS scrutiny. The *Internal Revenue Code* and related regulations allow three pricing methods considered arm's length: (1) the *comparable uncontrolled price method,* better known as market price; (2) the *resale price method,* sales price received for the property by the reseller less an appropriate markup; and (3) the *cost-plus method,* better known as cost-based transfer price. These three methods are the most commonly used methods throughout the world. Other methods are allowed if the MNC can show that they approximate arm's length.

Even though the United States has comprehensive transfer pricing rules, it remains difficult to determine the proper pricing method, and there are many issues over which taxpayers and the IRS can, and do, disagree. It is a well-accepted fact that more and more MNCs' transfer pricing practices are being investigated by national taxing authorities, adding uncertainties and risks to MNC investment and strategic planning.

Many companies are considering using advanced pricing agreements (APAs) as a means of reducing this uncertainty. Exhibit 10–8 provides a listing of the advantages and disadvantages of these agreements. An APA is a binding agreement between the taxpayer and the IRS on a transfer pricing method for certain international transactions. In 1998, 51 APAs were signed representing the largest one-year total since the program began in 1991. The IRS has recently streamlined the process to make APAs more accessible to smaller businesses. Canada also has a formal APA program in place.

EXHIBIT 10–8   Advantages and Disadvantages of Advanced Pricing Agreements

---

Advantages

Gives companies the opportunity to obtain prior approval of their transfer pricing policies
   from the IRS and foreign tax authorities.

Agreement is binding and the company will not be subject to further inquiries.

Certainty of treatment makes long-term strategic planning easier.

Useful in cases with unusual facts or circumstances that affect the profitability of an
   intercompany transaction.

Useful if the company implements a method not specified in Section 482 regulations of
   the IRS.

Disadvantages

Forces a company to disclose sensitive (confidential) information.

Lack of flexibility in adjusting transfer pricing policies.

Requires substantial documentation and administration, and requires professional
   expertise.

Complex, lengthy, and costly to comply with and to implement.

CONCLUSION

We have reviewed some of the objectives of MNC international taxation and
transfer pricing. Accomplishing the objectives of transfer pricing is difficult without considering the applicable tax laws. These objectives are so important at times
that they take precedence over the objectives of management control and performance evaluation. However, all are components of the strategic planning system
and work toward the optimal achievement of a multinational corporation's comprehensive international plan.

REVIEW QUESTIONS

1. How does the MNC's attitude toward business practices (ethnocentric, polycentric, or geocentric) affect the choice of a transfer pricing method?

2. How do corporate income taxes affect the strategic planning and control systems of MNCs?

3. Use Exhibit 10–1 to develop a list of information you would need about Taiwan to establish an effective transfer price for goods going in and out.

4. Compare and contrast the role of transfer pricing in a domestic versus a multinational corporation?

5. Identify the current choices an MNC has to set transfer prices, and discuss the
   advantages/disadvantages of each

6. The Internal Revenue Service cares about the use of arm's-length transfer prices. Why? Is the United States the only country that monitors transfer prices of imports and exports?

7. What is an advanced pricing agreement? What is its purpose? Do you expect to see more or less APAs in the future?

CASES

10–1 Can Spain Make the Top Ten?

Mary Miller is an American living in Madrid. After earning her MBA at the University of Oregon, she moved to Spain. That was 20 years ago. She speaks fluent Spanish, enjoys sangria and the bullfights, and dances the tango. She works in the central office of economic development for the Spanish government. One of her biggest challenges is to identify imaginative and effective incentive programs that will bring multinational corporation headquarters and/or foreign subsidiaries of foreign MNCs to Spain. She has read the survey that Deloitte Touche Tohmatsu International (DTTI) published on the various tax incentives available in European Union countries and finds the absence of the mention of Spain troubling. After all, Spain's corporate income tax rate is only 34 percent, lower than Belgium and the same as Denmark; both countries made the top 10 list for best-known tax incentives in the European Union. Mary Miller wants Spain on this list. So she pays Terry Browne, European Tax Director for DTTI, a visit. Terry says, "If EU countries wish to boost their attractiveness from a tax point of view, they need a strong marketing policy and tax laws beneficial to a broad range of industries in a variety of situations."

Questions

1. Develop a list of incentives, tax and nontax, that Mary Miller might explore to entice businesses to invest in Spain. Next to each incentive, provide a brief explanation of the benefit the incentive will provide to businesses.

2. From your master list in question 1, select a package of three incentives that Mary will market to the global business community.

3. Develop an outline of a marketing plan that Mary will present to Spain's economic ministers at their next board meeting. Hint: Keep in mind Terry Browne's words of wisdom.

10–2 Cash Is King

You are the manager of a Korean subsidiary of a U.S.-based MNC. Your subsidiary has been operating quite profitably during the last year, and you have excess cash to invest. You expect to use this cash to strengthen your subsidiary's position in Korea and ultimately to make your performance look exceptionally good. Your subsidiary buys raw materials from other Pacific Rim subsidiaries of the U.S.-based parent to manufacture its product. You also have had permission to buy these parts from the competition if you can get a better price. Lately, you have been buying from the competition.

This morning, you had the following conversation with headquarters:

HQ:

We need cash transferred into France, and your Korean subsidiary has excess cash at the moment. We want you to facilitate the movement of these funds by Friday.

You:

You know that today is Monday?

HQ:

Yes, we know that it is Monday.

You:

How do you propose that I accomplish your request, considering the fact that my government has just stopped all movement of excess cash out of the country?

HQ:

That could be a problem. You know your country's system. Work around it. France needs the cash by Friday.

Questions

1. How could you facilitate the flow of cash from Korea to France, given the present restrictions in Korea?
2. If you are unsuccessful in transferring funds to France, how else could the parent facilitate this flow?
3. Why is your subsidiary allowed to operate so independently (i.e., investing its own excess cash where it chooses and buying raw materials from the least expensive source)?
4. What is meant by the phrase, "You know the system"?

10–3 Ah! The Tangled Webs We Weave

Seated around a table are Gerhard Schmidt, German by nationality, and president of IBT-Europe; Neleh Nonreg, British, and vice president of finance; and Kathy McGuire, American, and vice president in charge of sales. IBT is a U.S.-based MNC that manufactures minicomputers. IBT-Europe is a very profitable, wholly owned subsidiary. As a result of its profitability, the president is given a great deal of autonomy from the parent company. Schmidt manages eight geographically organized subsidiaries that are treated as profit centers when it comes to control and evaluation. Budgets are set in terms of pretax profit and local managers are largely evaluated on their ability to "beat the numbers." Transfer prices are determined at the annual budget meeting, where all subsidiary managers have input. If a complicated tax situation arises, headquarters steps in and determines prices. The following conversation takes place:

McGuire:

> I received word from Ireland that the computers are en route to France at a price of $65,000. But France does not want to clear them through customs at this price, because machines from Belgium have been arriving at $55,000 and from the U.S.A. at $57,000. France wants a revised price from Ireland of $55,000.

Nonreg:

> Let's lower the price. It's only bookkeeping. We don't want the European Union investigating our transfer prices.

Schmidt:

> We can't lower the price. The whole point is to take advantage of the favorable tax deal we struck with Ireland. We have 12 years left on our exemption from income tax on all export sales. I thought this was all settled. We are in business to earn a profit.

Questions

1. What is going on here? Identify as many issues as you can.
2. Is this a centralization/decentralization problem?
3. Is minimizing payments to foreign governments an issue?
4. Can you suggest a solution?

ADDITIONAL READINGS

Bodner, P. "International Taxation." In *International Accounting and Finance Handbook.* 2nd ed., ed. F. D. S. Choi, New York: John Wiley & Sons, 1997, pp. 39: 1-21.

Borkowski, S. C. "Factors Affecting Transfer Pricing and Income Shifting: between Canadian and U.S. Transnational Corporations." *The International Journal of Accounting* 32, no. 4 (1997), pp. 391–415.

Carter, W. K.; D. M. Maloney; and M. H. VanVranken. "The Problems of Transfer Pricing." *Journal of Accountancy,* July 1998, pp. 37–40.

Cravens, K. S., and W. T. Shearon. "An Outcome-Based Assessment of International Transfer Pricing Policy." *The International Journal of Accounting* 31, no. 4 (1996), pp. 419–43.

O'Connor, W. "International Transfer Pricing." In *International Accounting and Finance Handbook.* 2nd ed., ed. F. D. S. Choi, New York: John Wiley & Sons, 1997, pp. 38: 1-38.

Ogum, G., and K. A. Kim. "New U.S. International Pricing Regulations." *Multinational Business Review,* Spring 1995, pp. 8–13.

Organization for Economic Cooperation and Development. *Taxing International Business: Emerging Trends in APEC and OECD Economies.* Paris: OECD, 1997.

Price Waterhouse. *Corporate Taxes: A Worldwide Summary.* New York: Price Waterhouse World Firm Services BV, Inc., 1996.

Tran, A. V., and T. M. Porcano. "Effective Tax Rates of Australian Companies: Industry and Size Effects." *Pacific Accounting Review* 9, no. 2 (1997), pp. 1–36.

Yancey, W. F., and K. S. Cravens. "A Framework for International Tax Planning for Managers." *Journal of International Accounting Auditing and Taxation* 7, no. 2 (1998), pp. 251–72.

INDEX

NOTES: